BLESSING

BLESSING and battles!

Reflections on the blessing of God and the battles of life.

S. Robert Maddox

BLESSING

Published by Redefining Faith Resources

Cover: Vietnam War military camouflage colors

Scripture quotations are from The Holy Bible, English Standard Version® (ESV®), copyright © 2001 by Crossway, a publishing ministry of Good News Publishers. Used by permission. All rights reserved.

Copyright © 2015 by S. Robert Maddox

No portion of this publication may be reproduced, stored in a retrieval system or transmitted in any form by any means - except for brief quotations in published reviews - without the prior written permission of the author.

ISBN: 978-0-9903912-4-1

DEDICATION

To Brenda, my wife.

We have been blessed with many blessings,
and when battles arose out of the blessings, you
quickly locked arms with me and gave loving aid.

CONTENTS

Foreword	Paul Handshue	1
Introduction	Where were you?	5
Part I	*Blessing of God*	11
Chapter 1	Pursue	13
Chapter 2	Prepare	25
Chapter 3	Parameters	37
Chapter 4	Posture	49
Part II	*Battles of Life*	61
Chapter 5	Praise	63
Chapter 6	Prevail	75
Chapter 7	Peace	87
Chapter 8	Perspective	99
Chapter 9	Prosperity	111
Chapter 10	Priorities	125
Chapter 11	Paradise	135

Epilogue	Fear not	147
Bonus Feature	Mount of Blessing	149
	Acknowledgement	161
	About the Author	163
	Books by the Author	165

FOREWORD

One of life's greater blessings, bestowed by God, are special friends. Such is the case for me with Bob Maddox. We first met in 1970 when stationed at Ellsworth Air Force Base, just outside Rapid City, South Dakota. We were young Christians struggling to find our place in the Lord's kingdom and needing a good home church; a group of sincere believers to aid us in our spiritual growth.

We attended Bethel Assembly of God; a church where a mighty move of God and revival was sweeping through the youth group. A passion was ignited in both our hearts for the things of the Kingdom. We were also blessed to meet and marry beautiful Spirit-filled women from this church.

The Lord led both of us to follow Him on different paths. Bob, and his wife Brenda, sensed a call into ministry and left the Air Force to attend

Bible College. To this day, a special love for those in military service continues in his heart. My wife Dawn and I continued in an Air Force career.

In the military, there are dream assignments where you feel, "I can't believe I'm getting paid to be here and experience this!" Then come the hard times – months filled with loneliness, fear, and exhaustion, as well as separation from family and loved ones. You think, "They aren't paying me enough to do this!" You pray, "Lord, keep me safe and help me!"

Bob speaks from experience about the similarities in *service* and *sacrifice* associated with military life and the Kingdom of God. Many learned military disciplines have enhanced the spiritual growth of his family and the various ministries he led.

Ask anyone serving in the Armed Forces about the three qualities held in highest esteem and you will hear, "Honor, Courage, and Integrity." Bob has walked the path of life's ebb and flow relying on these core values.

If you are struggling with battles in your life and wondering, "Where are the blessings of God?" or, "When will liberation come?" read the book and cling to God's promises. You will discover that in any situation, no matter how daunting and overwhelming, God is constantly at work leading you into spiritual rest and eternal victory.

Paul Handshue
Senior Master Sergeant, Retired
The United States Air Force

S. ROBERT MADDOX

INTRODUCTION

WHERE WERE YOU?

When I was a young teenager, President John F. Kennedy was murdered in Dallas, Texas. The nation was stunned. For the next several years the question asked was, "Where were you when you heard Kennedy was assassinated?"

Shocking events cause people to remember what they were doing when they hear about it. The trauma of tragedy makes the memory extra sensitive and highly focused.

I was in a Junior High classroom when the story hit the airwaves. Class ended; students were sent home. Mom was sitting in the living room watching the news. America came to a standstill for the next few days. Information and additional events surrounding the story continued to unfold.

Televisions were hardly turned off. His death left an indelible mark on my generation. For many, November 22, 1963, was a life-altering moment.

The same can be said about the current generation and September 11, 2001. Where were you when you heard the news of the terrorist attacks on New York and Washington DC, the senseless brutality by heartless thugs? How did you feel seeing the collapse of the World Trade Center and the damage to the Pentagon? What went through your mind hearing about the death of innocent men and women in buildings, on streets, and at a lonely country field?

My ministry included statewide church leadership at the time. I left early on *9/11* for a meeting at the state headquarters. I normally spent the five-hour road trip in prayer and meditation, the radio turned off.

Upon arrival, I entered the office but no one seemed present. I searched and found the staff gathered around a television in the break room. I made a cheerful entrance but received only sad stares. I asked, "What's going on?" Someone replied, "America is under attack!"

The youth minister in the church where I gave oversight scheduled a community-wide outreach that evening. Early in the afternoon, he called and asked if he should cancel. Coming together was the very thing people needed. I encouraged him to host the event. The turnout was great and there were meaningful results.

The following Sunday, church services were well attended. Some came to mourn the victims of terrorism; others came to confront their own mortality. Everyone wanted God's blessing.

Soon afterward, signs started appearing on billboards, automobiles, and houses saying, "God bless America!" The patriotic song with the same title became a standard at various events, often with United States flags waving high. People were looking for divine blessing while preparing to enter the battle against terrorism, which makes perfect sense. Who in their right mind would go into combat without the favor of the Lord?

Life involves numerous conflicts. What is often overlooked is the direct connection between blessing and battles—battles can be a sign of blessing.

If you are not blessed, you are ignored and considered insignificant; nobody wants what you have or cares what you say. Yet, the finger of God seen in a life often produces turbulence, turmoil, and tribulation. Envy, greed and lust officially declare war on the blessed and seek their downfall.

Could your immediate troubles be marking you as blessed of God? Are your battles an outgrowth of being blessed?

Or, when facing conflict, do your actions have the blessing of God upon them? Have you ever wondered, or even asked the Lord, if He sanctions your behavior?

Several stories given in the older covenant, as well as a couple mentioned in the New Testament, provide lessons about blessing and battles. This book, divided into two parts, gives various reflections on the blessing of God and the battles of life.

My hope is for these meditations to provide added confidence and courage for whatever lies ahead for you.

BLESSING and Battles

S. ROBERT MADDOX

In training

On mission

Part One

THE BLESSING
of God

*The LORD bless you and keep you;
the LORD make his face to shine upon
you and be gracious to you;
the LORD lift up his countenance upon
you and give you peace.
(Numbers 6:24-26)*

S. ROBERT MADDOX

CHAPTER ONE

PURSUE

Jabez was more honorable than his brothers; and his mother called his name Jabez, saying, "Because I bore him in pain." Jabez called upon the God of Israel, saying, "Oh that you would bless me and enlarge my border, and that your hand might be with me, and that you would keep me from harm so that it might not bring me pain!" And God granted what he asked. (1 Chronicles 4:9-10)

After my father died, my mother wanted help deciding what to do with his personal belongings. I told her I would come home later in the year and lend a hand sorting and disposing of unwanted items. While driving to Seattle, I spent a night at my brother's house in Montana.

Attending church was not part of our

upbringing. To my knowledge, none of the family members ever made a profession of faith in Christ. That evening our conversation went to religion, a rare topic among the siblings.

He told me about the last time he set foot in a church building. Wanting his daughters to be baptized, as he had been, arrangements were made for a traditional baptismal service in a denominational church. He became mildly unsettled by the focus of the worship service.

The topic of the sermon was God's blessing. The congregants were told to write *blessing requests* on pieces of paper, which were then read publicly. All the wishes were similar—wealth, or bigger and nicer homes. God was solicited for *things*.

A niece decided to make a request. Looking over her shoulder, my brother saw her asking for a friend to possess more money. He stopped her immediately, saying, "You can ask God to bless a church or the nation, but you may not ask Him to give people things." In the terminology of the religious, he saw the activity as excessively carnal.

After leaving his house to continue my travels, I reflected on the concept of asking for blessings. Done selfishly, requests for favors do have an element of egoism and can even tarnish devotion to

God.

Failure to receive *greedy* desires even makes for flimsy excuses to not follow Jesus: "God, You didn't give me what I want, so what good is following You? You seemingly don't care about me, so why should I care about You?"

Jabez is one of the several individuals mentioned in First Chronicles. Moving quickly through the list of *begats*, additional information is given about a few people, including him. He is described as the son of pain, named after pain, and granted freedom from pain. The man goes down in infamy as someone calling out to the Lord, and God giving a clear response: "'Oh that you would bless me…!' And God granted what he asked."

Bruce Wilkinson wrote a best-selling book about prayer, highlighting Jabez's request, transforming the spiritual life of many. Yet only two verses in the entire Bible are associated with the man.

Why is his name mentioned in Scripture? One explanation could be to demonstrate God's desire to bless. But, to emphatically declare wealth is assured by praying a specific way, or by having a right confession, is not true.

Believers occasionally reflect on James 4:2:

"You do not have, because you do not ask." Do not stop there, keep reading and attach the next verse: "You ask and do not receive, because you ask wrongly, to spend it on your passions." (James 4:3)

In desperate situations, many find themselves begging, "Please God, I need Your blessing." Wanting a blessing is not wrong and God wants to bless, but what is the motive behind wanting His special favor?

Scripture records comments in Genesis, Leviticus, and Numbers that give a clearer understanding of pursuing the blessing of God.

The voice of God

"By myself I have sworn, declares the LORD, because you have done this and have not withheld your son, your only son, I will surely bless you, and I will surely multiply your offspring as the stars of heaven and as the sand that is on the seashore. And your offspring shall possess the gate of his enemies, and in your offspring shall all the nations of the earth be blessed, because you have *obeyed my voice*." (Genesis 22:16-18)

Genesis shows blessings require obeying the *voice* of God.

After a long and prosperous life, Abraham and Sarah were finally able to have a child in old age. During Isaac's teenage years, God appeared to Abraham, instructing him to sacrifice the young man on an altar. Anguish must have filled their hearts.

Is forfeiting family members really so surprising? Many parents today sacrifice their teenagers out of selfish ambition, money, or any number of personal pleasures. Some infants are dedicated to the Lord at a worship gathering but are forbidden to enter vocational ministry.

Abraham did not withhold Isaac. Those with a similar kind of faith hold nothing back. The blessings of God are designed to assist the advancement of His Kingdom, both in your life and in others.

Delores was a devoted follower of Jesus and loving mother of nine. One of her daughters sensed a call into missionary service. Even though anxious about the distance and danger possibly involved, she felt honored God wanted one of her children in overseas ministry. What someone lays claim to is not exclusively their own, including children.

Are you holding on to something so tightly that it is beginning to dominate? Be careful of a transfer of ownership.

My father purchased property on the Olympic peninsula of Washington state. Since he owned the place, he often felt *obligated* to spend time there. He went frequently, even when wanting to do something else. The land was his, but he became enslaved to it.

Every possession has the potential to bind. Peace of mind is experienced by not holding on to anything too firmly and keeping nothing back from God.

Church members in the town of Ephesus were challenged to work, doing something useful and having something to share with the needy. (Ephesians 4:28) One reason for personal income is to help others during difficult times, combating a sense of discouragement.

While attending Bible College, my wife and I faithfully participated in a local church. An elderly couple regularly invited young families from the congregation to their house for a Sunday meal. During our visit, they wanted us to tour their neat and tidy home. My wife made a passing comment about the beautiful bedspread in their bedroom. Nothing was mentioned about us having just a few modest belongings in an inexpensive apartment.

The previous day, while the woman was cleaning and making her bed, she sensed the Lord asking her, "If someone wanted your bedspread would you give it?" She thought the question odd but responded she was willing. When my wife complimented her, she determined the comforter was meant for us. Not wishing to give something used, she gave my wife enough money to buy a new one.

Out of a willingness to listen to the voice of God, and by knowing she was blessed to encourage others, she was not enslaved to possessions. Relinquish all rights to everything entrusted to you and gain freedom.

If not overly attached to stuff, possessions cannot dominate. If you do not see anything as being owned *by* you, nothing can be taken *from* you. Give everything to God before it gets all of you.

The word of God

"You shall *keep my Sabbaths* and *reverence my sanctuary*: I am the LORD. If you walk in my statutes and observe my commandments and do them, then I will give you your rains in their season.... I will give peace in the land, and you shall lie down, and none shall make you afraid ... I will turn to you and make you fruitful and multiply you and will confirm my covenant with you ... I will make my dwelling among you ... I will walk among you and will be your God...." (Leviticus 26:2-12)

Leviticus reveals blessings require obeying the *word* of God.

All the blessings mentioned in these verses are attached to requirements:

Honor God with your schedule. Keep time with God foremost in your life. His companionship is more important than careers, recreation, and leisure.

Reverence His presence. As the Lord tabernacles (dwells) with you, live humbly and honorably.

The blessings of God are connected to conforming into His image and likeness. A favorite verse of many reads, "Delight yourself in the Lord, and he will give you the desires of your heart." (Psalms 37:4). Some misinterpret and their prayers sound like, "I'm delighted with you God, so give me, give me, give me!"; a greedy prayer. Look again! If *His* delight is what *you* desire, then showers of blessing are poured out. He can easily give what is craved when your desires conform to His delight.

Obedience to His word brings divine conformity. Scripture is designed to be the foundation of human existence, minimizing the risk of sinning. (Psalm 119:11)

God does not give blessings when the danger of improper use is high. Lifestyle has an important role in receiving His blessing. The Lord is only honored by a righteous testimony.

The Bible is a mighty weapon for God, not artillery against Him. The following comments have been wrongfully prayed by professing Christians: "You said it; therefore, You have to do it! … You're a liar if You don't act in accordance with Your word! … It's in the Book so You must come through! … As a child of God, I stand upon my rights."

Armament can be self-destructive. Attacking God with Scripture is self-inflicting. Insisting He do more, give more, and perform your wants is lethally disrespectful. Selfish demands dishonor the Lord.

God owes nothing to anyone. A heavenly inheritance is gained solely by divine grace. Many place themselves in harm's way by losing a grateful and appreciative heart.

The move of God

"On the day that the tabernacle was set up, the cloud covered the tabernacle…. So it was always: the cloud covered it by day and the appearance of fire by night. And *whenever the cloud lifted* from over the tent, after that the people of *Israel set out*, and in the place *where the cloud settled down*, there the people of *Israel camped* ... If it continued for a day and a night when the cloud lifted they set out. Whether it was two days, or a month, or a longer time that the cloud continued over the tabernacle, abiding there, the people of Israel remained in camp and did not set out, but when it lifted they set out. At the command of the LORD they camped, and at the command of the LORD they set out." (Numbers 9:15-23)

Numbers reveal blessings require obeying the *move* of God.

Differences exist between demanding, "Bless what I'm doing!" and declaring, "I'll do what You're blessing!"

Reading the wilderness journey causes a sense of *no rhyme to reason* for their travels. They went when He went and stayed when He stayed. Provisions were dependent on being close to the Lord.

Everyone has moments when they seem to be wandering, yet the blessing of God is dependent upon staying close to Him, even when appearing aimless. Better to be camping with God by a dry riverbed than being where He is not present.

Part of receiving blessings is faithfulness to His

guidance. God blesses anyone sensitive to the leading of the Spirit; those willing to move with Him.

One familiar saying is: "If you don't feel as close to God as you once did, guess who moved?" Restate it with a slightly different twist: "If you want God's blessing, guess who must move?"

Pursuing a blessing

Moses wrote that experiencing blessings are connected to obeying the voice, word, and move of God. Release yourself from a possessive nature; give preference to living by the pattern of His word, providing testimony of His Lordship; be sensitive to the leading of the Holy Spirit.

The best blessing is given to the pure of heart—namely, seeing God. (Matthew 5:8) Align yourself closely to Him. He wants to bless you.

Prayer

The blessed life comes out of a love relationship with the Lord. Everybody comes up short of deserving His blessings. Actually, everyone deserves His wrath. Jesus came and made possible a life intimately linked with God. By grace through faith, everything can change for the better. Will you enter the journey into abundant living? You can ask God for a newfound meaningful connection right now.

"Our heavenly Father, I recognize my failings and transgressions and ask for Your forgiveness. Wash away all my rebellion and pride. Change me into Your image and likeness.

"Lord Jesus, thank you for providing the way to peace and eternal life. Lead me, guide me, and show me how to live in abundant grace.

"Holy Spirit, strengthen me each day to reflect Jesus as my Lord. Help me know Your voice over all the various influencers demanding greater attention. Give me the courage to stand for truth and righteousness. Amen!"

CHAPTER TWO
PREPARE

So the taskmasters and the foremen of the people went out and said to the people, "Thus says Pharaoh, 'I will not give you straw. Go and get your straw yourselves wherever you can find it, but your work will not be reduced in the least.'" So the people were scattered throughout all the land of Egypt to gather stubble for straw ... And the foremen of the people of Israel, whom Pharaoh's taskmasters had set over them, were beaten and were asked, "Why have you not done all your task of making bricks today and yesterday, as in the past?" Then the foremen of the people of Israel came and cried to Pharaoh, "Why do you treat your servants like this? No straw is given to your servants, yet they say to us, 'Make bricks!' ... But he said, "You are idle, you are idle; that is why you say, 'Let us go and sacrifice to the LORD.' Go now and work. No straw will be given you, but you must still deliver the same number of bricks." The foremen of the people of Israel saw that they were in trouble.... They met Moses and Aaron, who were waiting for them, as they came out from Pharaoh; and they said to them, "The LORD look on you and judge, because you have made us stink in the sight of Pharaoh and his servants, and have put a sword in their hand to kill us." Then Moses turned to the LORD and said, "O Lord, why have you done evil to this people? Why did you ever send me? For since I came to Pharaoh to speak in your name, he has done evil to this people, and you have not delivered your people at all." (Exodus 5:10-23)

Believers should *pursue* the Lord's blessing, which comes from sensitivity to the voice, the word, and the move of God. His hand of blessing is seen when giving freely of His bounty, faithfully abiding under the umbrella of His presence, and making Him famous for His guidance. Know His voice, obey His word, and move with Him.

Receiving a blessing involves *preparation*. Although Jabez desired to not experience pain, some blessings only come after pain. Jabez's mother gave him his name saying, "I gave birth to him in pain." Are you presently experiencing the birth pains of blessing?

Understanding the first part of Exodus requires a broader look at the circumstances. Exodus 1 records the Egyptians forgetting past experiences, the Hebrew Joseph and his wisdom. Exodus 2 states God did not forget the promise given to His people. Exodus 3 mentions the Lord telling Moses that Israel would be blessed in a way never seen before. Yet, Exodus 4 presents an enigma: God sees the affliction but plans to harden the heart of Pharaoh, who will arrogantly refuse to release them.

Exodus 5 shows the stubbornness of the ruler and the increased trouble for the slaves. Israelis scorned Moses and he ends up questioning his leadership, as well as God's strategy. Even a *burning bush experience* does not stop questions about divinely orchestrated events.

Are you presently in an equally turbulent situation, finding yourself wondering what God is doing? Is there a purpose for you experiencing your troubles?

Coming together

A keyword to Israel's deliverance is *together*. Not everyone agreed about leaving Egypt. In the wilderness, the people clearly communicated their personal desire, saying to Moses, "Didn't we say to you in Egypt, 'Leave us alone….'" (Exodus 14:12)

Many have a Hollywood-fantasy concept about enslavement in Egypt, with a renowned actor playing the role of Moses. Correct the picture! By the time of their deliverance, Israelis had lived in Egypt for approximately *350* years.

Generally, everyone prefers to conform and imitate. People usually become like those around them. While living in Montana, I wore western clothing. Although not my natural or preferred style, the look seemed appropriate in a very cowboy environment.

Joseph was groomed and outfitted as an Egyptian. After just a couple of decades, his brothers did not recognize him when they arrived in the country.

Joseph's language was full of Egyptian expressions. He became fluent in the local idioms of the language.

Distinct differences exist between how people talk throughout the United States. Brenda and I were attending some meetings in San Antonio, Texas. While ordering lunch, the waitress asked about our beverage selection. My wife wanted to know what kind of "pop" they offered. The girl responded, "Y'all from the North aren't ya? Down here we call it soda-water."

Many growing up in the South lose southern slang after moving North, and some from the North quickly pick up a southern drawl when residing in the South.

Joseph's diet was basically Egyptian. The nutritional plan for God's people was established centuries later, while heading toward the Promise Land. Israelis even wished and longed for Egyptian food while wandering in the wilderness.

Except for certain privileges being denied, Israelis thought and acted like Egyptians. Three times in the wilderness journey they wanted to go back *home*, to the customary way of life. (Exodus 16:3, 17:3, Numbers 11:5)

In every society, people blend in to fit in. The history of the Jewish race shows an ethnic group adapting to the culture of their residency, whether Egypt, Babylon, Persia, or beyond.

Many may still remember the intense struggle between white and black nationals in South Africa when a longstanding injustice was finally addressed. The news media portrayed the whites as European, but the whites saw themselves as South Africans. The continent and customs of Africa were all they knew; England was foreign to them. They were South Africans with a European ancestral past.

After centuries of living in Egypt, the outlook, lifestyle, and mannerism of the Hebrew people was deeply influenced by their surroundings. They were basically North Africans with a Near Eastern lineage.

Sadly, some Israelis were quite content being slaves. Without downplaying or minimizing the inhumanity and cruelty of enslavement, were some aspects considered benefits?

They had *job security*. There was always work.

Basic needs of life were given without cost. Regular meals and lodging were provided.

Career advancement was possible. Smart and hardworking slaves could be promoted to project supervisors, domestic laborers, or personal attendants. Some positions required good grooming, nice clothing, and fine dining.

Pharaoh was not necessarily being flippant by accusing them of idleness, being lazy. Forced labor can make a person mentally sluggish and indifferent. Under these circumstances, a person is more concerned about meeting quotas instead of increasing productivity; motivated to do minimal work rather than achieve higher levels of excellence.

G. I.

The closest thing to forced labor I experienced was military life. No one can quit the Armed Forces. You are *Government Issue*.

I moved up the ranks of promotion rapidly, with minimum time-in-grade. Near the end of my enlistment, pressure came to reenlist. I asked a couple of *lifers* (career military personnel) why they stayed in the Air Force. One of the more interesting replies was, "I'm too lazy to work."

One Airman told me about a day when he did not feel like working. He picked up a clipboard from a nearby desk and casually walked around the squadron hangar, occasionally stopping and appearing to write something important. He spent his entire shift in mindless activity, and not one person ever asked what he was doing.

In military life, *looking* busy often prevented being asked to do something. A person could fly silently under the radar, undetected, and receive a regular paycheck without much effort. Was the thinking and attitude of some Hebrews any different?

Israelis were not in total agreement about the shape and design of the much-needed deliverance. They were not prepared to receive God's perfect blessing.

Preparation

God made a promise and the time was right to claim their inheritance, but Israel needed to learn the blueprint of His blessing. Some remembered their heritage, but not everyone. A few cursed their ancestry for keeping them back from the privileges of citizenship. Many were not looking for freedom *from* Egypt, but freedom *to become* Egyptians.

How do you change the heart of people accepting and finding solace in their predicament? How do you get people to quit being comfortable in circumstances? How do you shake people out of complacency over their plight? They must feel the harshness of a taskmaster. Make Egyptians odious and put pressure on the Hebrews to prefer going elsewhere.

Troublesome circumstances made Israel see the need for freedom. Pharaoh became a means of bringing *mutual agreement* to God's people, moving them into one accord. Tribulation produces oneness; common causes bring people closer together.

Process

The first step in preparing for a blessing is *unity*.

The process started by the Hebrews finding consensus against the divinely appointed leader, feeling upset and disappointed with Moses. (V.21) Anger towards Moses exposed their true spiritual condition. The carnality of Egypt had become deeply entrenched in their lives.

Israelis thought only of their personal well-being, not divine promises. They needed a special awakening to God's eternal plan. The reaction toward Moses showed a people needing a change of heart before a conversion of circumstances.

How did Moses feel?

"God, you called me to help these people and things have only gotten worse."

"Lord, would you mind defining the term *rescue* for me?"

The second step in preparing for a blessing is *correct perceptions* about the source of the problem, moving from agreement *against Moses* into harmony *against Egypt*. The pestilence and plagues became the turning point. With the country in ruins, becoming Egyptian became less inviting. After the land was ravaged, the Promise Land was accurately seen as full of *milk* and *honey*.

A correct and clear focus prepares people for a blessing.

A wayward world

Are you going through a difficult time and questioning God? Are you resenting leadership and blaming others for your circumstances? If you are going to be angry, get mad at carnality. A faulty worldview prevents the ability to receive His blessing.

If it takes tribulation to get you moving into His blessing, why despise it? I am not suggesting you fail to acknowledge the uncomfortable nature of the situation, but why hate it? Life in a rebellious world is not designed without trials.

Troubles shape and prepare you to move into His promises. God has not left you but is overseeing every activity. He is organizing and coordinating your total development, making you like Jesus, and preparing you for special benefits and perfect blessings.

On the other side of tribulation is an extravagant inheritance. Is there a blessing just waiting for your readiness? Are you thoroughly prepared for a season of refreshing? The Lord has a sea to divide, daily manna to give, and a rock to break open. He has an eternal heritage to bestow, yet only if you are willing to go beyond a lifeless form of living.

Low moments

Low moments occur in every occupation – times of perplexity, puzzlement, despair, and discouragement. Call it by any name but it is simply a low moment.

Early in ministry, I experienced a major disappointment. I was inwardly struggling and feeling miserable, emotionally frayed. My nerves were worn thin.

My wife held me up in prayer but neither of us seemed to have answers. I decided to write a longtime mentor, someone very instrumental in my early spiritual training.

He had not heard from me for quite some time. Pouring every thought and feeling into the contents of the letter may have shocked him. He wrote back, "Although I don't fully comprehend what you're experiencing, it is obvious you're extremely wounded. As your faith in God must mature, so your ministry must ripen. God is cultivating your fruitfulness. Trust Him!"

To state it bluntly, during trouble, *GROW UP*.

Find benefit in whatever comes, allowing it to shape you for a blessing. Many promises are fulfilled only after momentary afflictions. (1 Peter 4: 12-14)

CHAPTER THREE
PARAMETERS

The same night he arose and took his two wives, his two female servants, and his eleven children, and crossed the ford of the Jabbok. He took them and sent them across the stream, and everything else that he had. And Jacob was left alone. And a man wrestled with him until the breaking of the day. When the man saw that he did not prevail against Jacob, he touched his hip socket, and Jacob's hip was put out of joint as he wrestled with him. Then he said, "Let me go, for the day has broken." But Jacob said, "I will not let you go unless you bless me." (Genesis 32:22-26)

"When my angel goes before you and brings you to the Amorites and the Hittites and the Perizzites and the Canaanites, the Hivites and the Jebusites, and I blot them out, you shall not bow down to their gods

nor serve them, nor do as they do, but you shall utterly overthrow them and break their pillars in pieces. You shall serve the LORD your God, and he will bless your bread and your water, and I will take sickness away from among you. None shall miscarry or be barren in your land; I will fulfill the number of your days. I will send my terror before you and will throw into confusion all the people against whom you shall come, and I will make all your enemies turn their backs to you. And I will send hornets before you, which shall drive out the Hivites, the Canaanites, and the Hittites from before you. I will not drive them out from before you in one year, lest the land become desolate and the wild beasts multiply against you. Little by little I will drive them out from before you, until you have increased and possess the land. (Exodus 23:23-30)

Blessed be the God and Father of our Lord Jesus Christ, who has blessed us in Christ with every spiritual blessing in the heavenly places. (Ephesians 1:2-3)

Everyone should *pursue* and needs to *prepare* to receive God's blessing. He desires to bless His people, but some blessings come through the doorway of trouble. If it takes friction to get people moving into His blessing, then so be it.

What are the *parameters* of God's blessing? Are

there boundaries to His promises? Some people have limited their focus, restricting what qualifies as a blessing. Paul instructs the church that the Lord blesses with "every spiritual blessing in the heavenly places," yet many only want tangible blessings in the earthly realm.

The ultimate blessing is mercy, a kindness that covers the magnitude of rebellion and pride. Followers of Jesus are greatly blessed with a good standing before God, where genuine peace, joy, and love reside. Should a person lack earthly substance, they are still wonderfully blessed abiding in Christ.

Do not misunderstand! God does bless His people in tangible ways. The Lord is about compassion. Nations experience many generous benefits where Jesus is embraced. In comparison to the rest of humanity, health care, education, alleviation of human indignity, and injustice are more consistently advocated by Christ-followers.

The Lord sincerely cares about your present well-being. He abides in the hearts of believers, sensing hurt, experiencing joy, loving laughter and removing tears.

Old Testament Jacob needed a divine encounter one night, a wrestling match that knocked a hip out of the socket. He persisted through the gloomy darkness and prevailed until the morning light. Like the old patriarch, many experience fears by various circumstances and even end up lame wrestling with anxiety, yet divine blessings shine greatest when frailty is most evident.

The message of Jesus elevates weakness to a position of strength. Some religions highlight force and advocate crushing vulnerability. Faith in God champions strength through humility.

"Bless the LORD, O my soul, and all that is within me, bless his holy name! Bless the LORD, O my soul, and forget not all his benefits, who forgives all your iniquity, who heals all your diseases, who redeems your life from the pit, who crowns you with steadfast love and mercy, who satisfies you with good so that your youth is renewed like the eagle's." (Psalm 103:1-5) Recipients of divine benefits are the foremost pursuers of God and seek only Him.

What does Scripture reveal about the limits of God's blessing?

Scope of blessing

Abundant promises are held in reserve for God's people.

The Lord provides the necessities of life. The

Sermon on the Mount showcased the detail and depth of God's concern. Jesus spoke of the number of hairs on a head, but the emphasis was more than just quantity—He was highlighting particular hairs. When hair goes down a drain, people usually focus on the total number, but the Lord notices which one: "There goes hair number 2013, 1046, 3029...."

Jesus also reminded the crowd that birds do not sow yet have adequate provisions, and lilies do not toil but have great splendor. God gives what is necessary and what lavishly serves as a blessing.

After the birth of our second child, our compact car no longer met the household need. My first impulse was to buy a full-size vehicle, but we sensed divine guidance toward a more affordable mid-size automobile. The Lord understands the need for adequate and trustworthy transportation, but what is affordable?

Some people mistakenly act and hope God will bail them out. Blessings involve gaining direction from the Lord *prior* to making decisions. A fine line exists between blessings and burdens.

The Lord provides opportunities for advancement. Divine guidance often leads to golden opportunities. The prophet Daniel chose to live righteously in a society demanding compromise. He withstood the pressures of Babylon and became second-in-command.

Do sale representatives have to behave shadily to close a deal? Must people work inordinate hours to experience success? The road to advancement is walking in His counsel.

The New Testament gives helpful guidance. First Thessalonians encourages *diligence* and *dedication*, not expecting something for nothing. Ephesians and Colossians give mention to the importance of *dependability*. Romans highlights the critical role of *direction* by the Spirit. Heed the word from the Lord about a sound work ethic and follow the divine pattern for blessings.

The Lord provides wisdom and insight. Followers of Jesus meditate on Scripture, ending up with dove-like innocence and serpent-like wisdom. The outcome of study is a knowledge about the follies of life, an ability to see behind various forms of craftiness, an insight on the frailties of the human nature, and an understanding of the evil warring against godliness.

The Bible contains great truths about life and is ageless with knowledge. The best of divine and human understanding is contained in 66 books, written by humans but authored by God. Reading newspapers, periodicals and books are helpful, but God's blessing is discovered in the *Book*.

Stipulations of blessings

First, what is best for your life? In the 1980's, various ministers gave a strong emphasis on earthly wealth. Believers were told, "You are a child of *a* king, a king's kid. You should live in opulence." One word was out of place: You are a child of *the* King.

King Jesus was despised and rejected of men. He had no place to lay His head. He gave instruction for His followers to take up a burdensome hideous instrument of death and live in a manner similar to Him. Living as *the* King's kid is abiding in the riches of righteousness.

The message of Jesus may not lead to material wealth but will usher in the majesty of His presence. He knows what is best and what will lend itself to divine transformation. His followers' assignment is to manifest the nature of Jesus regardless of circumstances or situations, good or bad.

Are you struggling with questions about an uncomfortable situation? Are you desperate for answers about what to do? Wrestle through every fear until you have God's approval. Spiritually tussling with traumatic situations and holding onto the Lord will indelibly transform your life.

Secondly, what are your motivations? What is the intent behind a blessing? Impurely serving God ushers in self-seeking ambitions. (1 Timothy 6:3-10)

God knows the true desires of the human heart. Motivation counts! Is His name being used to satisfy greed? Anyone feeling invincible and toying with selfishness ultimately loses.

Thirdly, divine promises come with "if" clauses. For example:

"For the eyes of the LORD run to and fro throughout the whole earth, to give strong support to those whose heart is blameless toward him." (2 Chronicles 16:9) *If* wholeheartedly attempting to live blamelessly before him, *then* strong support is promised.

"Since we have these promises, beloved, let us cleanse ourselves from every defilement of body and spirit, bringing holiness to completion in the fear of God." (2 Corinthians 7:1) *If* you cleanse yourself of every defilement, *then* heavenly wholeness is experienced.

The promises of God are based on a lifestyle reflective of Him, where heartbeat and breath are devoted solely to Him.

Sequence of blessings

What if God is fully trusted and all stipulations are met, yet you still lack a sense of blessing? Special promises must also meet His timetable! A blessing before its time does not bless. God may not be refusing but is simply wanting you to *wait*.

God promised Israel an inheritance *little by little*. Too much, too soon is burdensome. Preparedness gives an ability to recognize and appreciate a blessing.

Imagine a mega-church searching for a new pastor. A young graduate, fresh out of college, sends a resume. The pulpit committee, in a moment of insanity, invites the newly credentialed minister to present their ministry. The voting membership, in an equally bizarre case of craziness, selects the person.

Pastoring an extremely large congregation could easily devastate the well-being of someone still consumed with college idealism. They have not yet learned how to love people despite unsavory comments and criticism; they are not groomed to handle the occasional disparaging remark. Church members would be equally devastated by inexperienced leadership and would most likely encounter major setbacks.

Trying to force a blessing into existence, demanding or insisting upon a particular blessing, and attempting to get a blessing before properly trained, would be a burden. Blessings are designed to come gradually after management skills are developed.

When asking God for a specific blessing, ask yourself, "Am I ready?" As a person becomes more like Jesus, blessings become more feasible.

Abundance

The Lord abundantly blesses, bountifully providing provisions, advancement, and insight. But what is best for your life? Motives and timing are both critical. Great blessings often follow diligent waiting.

After Christmas, some people experience *down* feelings. How can the excitement before Christmas become so disappointing afterwards? The greater part of the Christmas celebration is the sense of anticipation. Similarly, the greater portion of God's blessing is time spent with Him during questioning moments.

The parameters of God's blessing are limitless,

but blessings involve terms and timing, preventing blessings from becoming burdens.

S. ROBERT MADDOX

CHAPTER FOUR
POSTURE

Jesus said to her, "Everyone who drinks of this water will be thirsty again, but whoever drinks of the water that I will give him will never be thirsty again. The water that I will give him will become in him a spring of water welling up to eternal life." (John 4:13-14)

On the last day of the feast, the great day, Jesus stood up and cried out, "If anyone thirsts, let him come to me and drink. Whoever believes in me, as the Scripture has said, 'Out of his heart will flow rivers of living water.'" Now this he said about the Spirit, whom those who believed in him were to receive, for as yet the Spirit had not been given, because Jesus was not yet glorified. (John 7:37-39)

The blessing of God involves pursuing, preparing and parameters. What is the correct *posture* for receiving His blessings? What frame of mind can the Lord bless?

John's narrative expresses two activities of the Holy Spirit: a spring *welling up* and a stream *flowing out*. Blessings are not designed to be preserved in a jar. Although personally pleasurable, blessings are not solely for individual enjoyment.

God blesses and satisfies every longing. Do you recognize His blessing? Do you comprehend the wealth of having sins forgiven? Through regret, remorse and repentance, He gives peace to troubled minds, contentment to anxious hearts, and healing to physical bodies. He wonderfully blesses those abiding and resting in Him.

Receiving blessings, however, is just half the story. He loves you *as well as* everyone else. From the Holy Spirit comes satisfying thirst *and* overflowing rivers of blessing. Filled with the Spirit, yet failing to overflow onto others, is a tragic mistake. Until spilling over on others, a believer cannot experience the abundance of blessing.

Christian humanism, where self is the center of attention and ambition, has become deeply ingrained into the lives of many claiming to follow Jesus. Some want blessings with total disregard to benefiting others.

Do you get excited at the thought of *sitting with* Jesus, but shun the thought of *living like* Jesus? Do you seek friendship with Jesus without being a friend to others? Can anyone honestly love God without loving people?

Satisfying personal thirst but bottling and concealing the life-giving stream fails the purpose of blessings. The right posture is *blessed to be a blessing*. By joining the twofold *fill/flow* mission of the Spirit, blessings are abundantly experienced.

Satisfaction is connected to the floodwaters of His nature bringing cleansing to attitudes, ambitions and actions, then aspiring to represent Jesus to the nations. Thirst is quenched in the overflow. Become associated with both the thirst-quenching spring and life-giving streams.

Many prefer being like Jesus exclusively in buildings designed for worship. The greater blessing occurs after leaving the place and giving testimony of Him. Worship occurring in dedicated facilities must go beyond the four walls and impact the world. By lining-up with the Great Commission (Matthew 28:18-20), the full measure of His promises is thirst quenching.

Sometimes pure efforts are misunderstood, honorable motives are questioned, and honest intentions are doubted. Should this prevent believers from being *Jesus with skin on*? No!

The Holy Spirit has come to manifest Jesus, who portrayed Himself in three ways.

An unassuming servant

The gospel writers record a story about a raging storm on the Sea of Galilee. (Matthew 4:35-41) The disciples became afraid while Jesus slept. Why did He act to calm the sea, for a better night's rest? He addressed the storm for the peace of mind of His friends. Jesus never altered circumstances for personal comfort.

Consider Jesus at Golgotha. What could He have done on the cross? A songwriter expressed, "He could have called ten thousand angels to destroy the world and set Him free…but He died alone for you and me."

In one of Paul's letters Jesus is described as being in the very nature of God yet making Himself nothing, taking the nature of a servant, humbling Himself, and becoming obedient to death. The paragraph begins by telling His followers to have the same attitude. (Philippians 2:5-11)

The *ambition* of a servant is *blessed to bless*; the

heart of a servant is *receiving to give*; the *spirit* of a servant may become *tired but never dampened.*

A dangerous mindset is expressed when saying, "Let somebody else do it!" or "Let somebody else take their turn!"

In one of my pastoral assignments, the nursery coordinator asked me one Sunday to highlight, in the worship gathering announcements, the need for more helpers in her ministry area. The three services each week required high numbers of volunteers. I took a few extra moments to emphasize the opportunity—encouraging and challenging but not demanding.

While greeting people afterward, a middle-aged woman decided to take issue with my comments. As an older mother, she took offense feeling *pressured* to help.

She said very indignantly, which is not a good way to speak to someone having just spent a considerable amount of energy passionately communicating the Good News, "I served my time in the nursery *[as if referring to jail]*, let the young mothers take their turn."

I was annoyed with her attitude and, unfortunately, was not in the best frame of mind. Before catching myself, I responded calmly and softly, "Let me see if I've got this straight. You're telling me you got the royal shaft when you were a young mother and you want to make sure these young mothers get the royal shaft, as well."

She gasped and said, "That's not what I said." I replied, "That's what it sounded like."

Afterward, I informed the deacons of my poor response. One jokingly thought I acted under a heavenly anointing. Thankfully, the woman continued attending the church, maintained our friendship, and even graciously signed up to help in the nursery one service a month.

A servant expects little or no tangible returns from their investment, whether in time, talent or treasures. Be on guard of only thinking or watching out for *numero uno*. Without a servant's heart selfishness is guaranteed to creep in, eliminating the potential of overflow and placing limitations on blessings.

A beacon of light

Living as a genuine follower of Jesus will be controversial in a society bent on selfishness. Devout followers naturally upset anyone preferring to compromise truth and remain on friendly terms with falsehood. A lifestyle of faith *should* offend those wishing to continue in rebellious bondage.

Peter wrote, "If you are insulted for the name of Christ, you are blessed, because the Spirit of glory and of God rests upon you." (1 Peter 4:14) When standing up for purity, morality, integrity, and righteousness, followers of Jesus will occasionally cause offense. Compromising people find those living wholesomely to be personally insulting. When a believer experiences victory where others are failing, some will feel demoralized instead of inspired and fail to pursue overcoming power.

Followers of Jesus cannot help when others become upset witnessing the light of grace. Yet, are some believers more *obnoxious* instead of *offensive,* attempting to *force* what can only be effective through the Holy Spirit?

An out-of-state group of volunteers was assisting an inner-city ministry at one of the more violent housing projects of Chicago. A young worker in the organization took a few of these helpers to pick up some necessary supplies. Teenagers from the neighborhood were standing on a street corner. As the van drove by them, the worker stuck his head out the window and yelled, "You're all going to hell!", scaring the volunteers. He was proud of condemning the neighborhood youth and considered his actions a viable witness. The conduct was more than just spiritually offensive; it was carnally obnoxious. He attempted to force divine conviction.

Similar destructive behavior is also a problem in faith communities. During my college years, Brenda and I were actively attending a local church. Some younger couples became upset with church leadership and decided to go elsewhere. We were receiving pressure to join them. They had a couple justifiable complaints, but their attitude was clearly obnoxious. A wrong heart never makes right actions. We decided to stay involved where we were and not be swayed by poor actions and bad manners. We lost a few friendships.

A retired missionary, active in the church, watched everything. He said to me later, "You will never regret your decision. You did right, and God will bless." His words came true. The Lord was very gracious to me throughout all my years in church leadership.

From an eternal perspective, you cannot lose when shining as a light of truth. In whatever choices you face, stand upright. You will be blessed.

A vessel of love

Some consider love *sentimental and soft*, yet the love of Christ is *compassionate but tough*. Genuine love does not support what Scripture does not condone. Do some tolerate and overlook shameful actions out of fear of losing personal accolades and special favors?

Love uncovers and puts an end to distortion, dishonesty, and deception. Love overlooks weakness, but never excuses wrong. Love exposes error, so problems can be brought to God for a solution. Does this cause a sense of awkwardness? Sometimes! Yet shining light on deceit is worth the remedy as grace rushes in and fills the emptiness of defiance.

If the Bible cannot accept a certain lifestyle, how can those with faith in God ignore inappropriate living? If the values people choose to live by will also bring failure, how can someone stand idly by and watch them end up ruined? Love does not sanction a person doing their *own* thing, but the *right* thing.

Love requires a heart of *compassion* made out of *leather*. You may be accused of being unkind, but you care too much to allow others to live falsely.

Full and overflow

More than seeking to be full, desire to overflow. The purpose of blessings is to bless. Be a servant, a beacon of truth and a vessel of authentic love. Imitate

Jesus and posture yourself for God's blessing. The result?

"The righteous flourish like the palm tree and grow like a cedar in Lebanon. They are planted in the house of the LORD; they flourish in the courts of our God. They still bear fruit in old age; they are ever full of sap and green, to declare that the LORD is upright; he is my rock, and there is no unrighteousness in him." (Psalm 92:12-15)

BLESSING and Battles

Graduation from Technical Training School

Me sitting on a Mace Missile

Part Two

THE BATTLES
of Life

Shadrach, Meshach, and Abednego answered and said to the king, "O Nebuchadnezzar, we have no need to answer you in this matter. If this be so, our God whom we serve is able to deliver us from the burning fiery furnace, and he will deliver us out of your hand, O king. But if not, be it known to you, O king, that we will not serve your gods...."
(Daniel 3:16-18)

CHAPTER FIVE

PRAISE

After this the Moabites and Ammonites, and with them some of the Meunites, came against Jehoshaphat for battle. Some men came and told Jehoshaphat, "A great multitude is coming against you from Edom, from beyond the sea; and, behold, they are in Hazazon-tamar" (that is, Engedi). Then Jehoshaphat was afraid and set his face to seek the LORD, and proclaimed a fast throughout all Judah. And Judah assembled to seek help from the LORD; from all the cities of Judah they came to seek the LORD. ... [King's prayer] *"O our God, will you not execute judgment on them? For we are powerless against this great horde that is coming against us. We do not know what to do, but our eyes are on you."*
... [Prophetical response] *"Listen, all Judah and inhabitants of Jerusalem and King Jehoshaphat:*

Thus says the LORD to you, 'Do not be afraid and do not be dismayed at this great horde, for the battle is not yours but God's.... You will not need to fight in this battle. Stand firm, hold your position, and see the salvation of the LORD on your behalf, O Judah and Jerusalem.' Do not be afraid and do not be dismayed. Tomorrow go out against them, and the LORD will be with you." Then Jehoshaphat bowed his head with his face to the ground, and all Judah and the inhabitants of Jerusalem fell down before the LORD, worshiping the LORD. And the Levites, of the Kohathites and the Korahites, stood up to praise the LORD, the God of Israel, with a very loud voice. ... And when he had taken counsel with the people, he appointed those who were to sing to the LORD and praise him in holy attire, as they went before the army, and say, "Give thanks to the LORD, for his steadfast love endures forever." And when they began to sing and praise, the LORD set an ambush against the men of Ammon, Moab, and Mount Seir, who had come against Judah, so that they were routed. For the men of Ammon and Moab rose against the inhabitants of Mount Seir, devoting them to destruction, and when they had made an end of the inhabitants of Seir, they all helped to destroy one another. ... Then they returned, every man of Judah and Jerusalem, and Jehoshaphat at their head, returning to Jerusalem with joy, for the LORD had made them rejoice over their enemies. (2 Chronicles

20:1-4, 12, 15, 17-19, 21-23, 27)

King Jehoshaphat became ruler of the southern nation of Judah at age 35 and reigned 25 years. In the sight of the Lord, his leadership was recognized as rightly done. He was on the threshold of a battle and his response was very normal—afraid.

There is no evil in sensing fear. Apprehension sometimes works to a person's advantage. Although anxious feelings are not evil, the response to fear must be honed on the anvil of God. A priestly prophet responded to the troubled ruler that *the battle is the Lord's*.

During a visit to the Total Living Network facility in Aurora, Illinois (Cable television TLN), I noticed the same words on a plaque sitting on the desk of Jerry Rose. The founder of the ministry, Owen Carr, labored through all the financial, political, and legal issues in Chicago to establish TV38, embracing this promise as a means of assurance.

Life has battles. Connected with the *blessing of God* are *battles of life*. Some attempt to deny conflicts, believing to acknowledge struggles contradicts faith. A well-known Christian personality said on television, "I have no battles because I am living in victory through Jesus," a cute and charming sound-bite with seemingly spiritual connotations, but not very Scriptural.

If you accept the Bible as the authoritative word of God, then you should recognize the world is in rebellion against the Creator. Followers of Jesus are part of the Lord's army and are in conflict with the spirit of the age and the satan, the evil nemesis of God. The ruler of darkness is fighting for the souls of mankind and the defeat of every believer.

The conflicts in life are more like the Vietnam War than World War II. In traditional wars, definite lines on a map show territory held by one side or the other. In Vietnam, local laborers working on military bases during the day could very well be enemy forces at night. The enemy was *everywhere* and could be *anyone*.

Followers of Jesus are in a fight upholding righteousness, but battle lines are not clearly drawn. The enemy *surrounds* those serving the Lord. Conflict can occur anywhere. Attempts are continually made to inflict casualties on sincere believers with the weapons of discouragement and compromise.

Jim and his family visited our church in Minnesota. He served as chairman of a religious organization and as a member of the Trustees Board at a large liturgical church. Even though an upright and religious man, he had yet to make a definitive commitment to follow Jesus.

He and his family showed up at church one Sunday and, liking what they experienced, became regular attendees. They eventually became members and gave hearty support. He sometimes accidentally referred to me as "Father," giving both of us a good laugh. His wife had no idea how to address a pastor's wife—never had one before.

Shortly after joining the church, various difficulties began occurring in his home. One of the children was diagnosed with Crones Disease; sections of his small intestines were eventually removed. Jim was laid-off at an Implement Dealership and struggled to find another sales position. When he finally gained employment, the new company applied pressure to perform questionable tactics; he thought it best to quit.

Jim and I went out for coffee one morning, and he said, "Pastor, nothing like this ever happened to me until I started attending your church." Can it be that before anyone becomes an earnest follower of Jesus there is no need for battles? No one who is living to serve themselves is a threat to the devil, even someone highly religious. But go AWOL from the enemy's influence and he attacks and attempts to destroy.

I replied to Jim, "Isn't it great being surrounded by people who are earnestly praying while all this is happening? Several are regularly petitioning the Lord, standing in the gap on your behalf as you travel through the valley of confusion. Was there any guarantee these struggles weren't going to happen? On the contrary, God knew what was ahead and brought you into an environment where you could more readily experience overcoming power."

If facing a fight, is your heart full of questions and fear? An incident in the life of a Judean king provides a workable strategy.

Enemy attack

Distant relatives had become longtime enemies and they combined forces to fight Israel. Oftentimes your worst foes are familiar to you, forces at one time in close kinship with you.

I smoked cigarettes for eleven years. Following Jesus means not serving two masters. Tobacco is a cruel taskmaster. By grace and divine strength, I quit the addiction, but the craving haunted me for years afterward. Habitual enemies do not give up easily.

For Judah, the enemy seemed to have the

victor's edge. Their army appeared superior and had the numerical advantage. Sin often feels the same way. The rebellious nature puts on an appearance of being more powerful.

Judah's situation had a sense of irony. As descendants of Esau and Lot, the Lord would not allow their destruction when Israel approached the Promise Land centuries earlier. Jehoshaphat even lodged a complaint: "God, if You knew this day was coming, why didn't You let us destroy them earlier? Why didn't You let us address the problem when we felt more confident and better equipped?"

The book of Judges reveals various groups living in the land were not destroyed during the conquest so the descendants of Israel, without prior battle experience, would learn warfare. (Judges 3:1-2)

Every generation of believers needs to become experienced combatants. Conflict is not designed to overwhelm but to teach the importance of *leaning on Jesus*. Battles help believers appreciate the blessing of just knowing God and living for eternity.

Jehoshaphat made fear work to his advantage, causing him to *seek the Lord*. Fear helped him recognize his shortcomings.

Deficiencies are bad if they generate a desire to throw in the towel and give up. Inadequacies are good if they cause a pursuit for divine strength and solutions. Jehoshaphat chose to depend on God and eventually gained answers.

Encouraging words

First encouragement: "Do not be afraid and do not be dismayed." Be strong of heart! Defeat starts by an absence of hope.

I was invited to speak at a well-established church that was going through some momentary trouble – nice people, nice facility, nice town. Upon entering the building, I recognized a sense of hopelessness. Change only starts by having *confidence* in God (from the Latin words *cum fide*, "with faith"). All things are possible to those who believe. No situation is beyond His reach.

Are family members not living for God? Hope in the Lord.

Are mom and dad talking about divorce? Things can change by divine grace.

Struggling with addictions and unwholesome desires? God is greater.

Suffering with a physical malady? God is the

Healer.

The Lord desires to calm your soul with nine encouraging words: "Do not be afraid, and do not be dismayed."

Second encouragement: "The battle is not yours, but God's." Give every conflict to the Lord. Do not try fighting what God has reserved for Himself. Recognize the conflict is real and get the Lord involved.

Eating disorder? The battle is the Lord's! A relationship problem at home or work? Release the situation into God's hands!

With *unwavering hope*, give the conflict to Jesus.

The fight

Waiting for solutions often seems endless and feels unbearable. God takes up the struggle, but you suffer the strain.

Nothing can be done to help the Lord except stay out of the way. You may feel an inner drive to step in and help, but how can anyone really help the *Almighty*?

Then what can you do? What did Jehoshaphat

and the people do? They audibly praised God! (Vs. 18-19) They fell down and worshiped, entering His presence with humility, and then stood to praise with *loud voices*.

People naturally become afraid by the sounds of battle. Drown out the noise of war by verbally rejoicing in the triumphant Lord. Vocalize praise until your heart hears only victory. Rather than focus on the struggle, concentrate on the Victor. They sang and praised, while God worked victory on the battlefield.

The Lord eventually won the conflict by causing the enemy to fight each other. Enemies are usually so hate-filled that they devour each other when they cannot destroy an opponent.

Scary

Battles are scary. In your inadequacy, seek the Lord, do not lose hope, and give Him the struggle. Make the following phrase a regular mantra: "The battle's ragin', but I'm still praisin'." There is no denying that battles are real but fill the air with shouts of triumph.

Tremendous joy comes when the battle is over. Israel returned "to Jerusalem with joy, for the Lord had given them cause to rejoice over their enemies."

(V. 27)

People sometimes think a battle will never end. Yes it will! No conflict lasts forever, and a special joy is reserved when the victory comes. Look for divine joy to quickly come your way.

God's victory comes by *focusing on Him* instead of the conflict; freedom comes when *giving Him* the battle instead of entering the fight; *praise Him* and drown out the noise of war.

S. ROBERT MADDOX

CHAPTER SIX

PREVAIL

The whole commandment that I command you today you shall be careful to do, that you may live and multiply, and go in and possess the land that the LORD swore to give to your fathers. And you shall remember the whole way that the LORD your God has led you these forty years in the wilderness, that he might humble you, testing you to know what was in your heart, whether you would keep his commandments or not. And he humbled you and let you hunger and fed you with manna, which you did not know, nor did your fathers know, that he might make you know that man does not live by bread alone, but man lives by every word that comes from the mouth of the LORD. Your clothing did not wear out on you and your foot did not swell these forty years. Know then in your heart that, as a man disciplines his son, the LORD your God disciplines you. So you shall keep the commandments of the LORD your God by walking in his ways and by fearing him. For the LORD your God is bringing you into a good land, a land of brooks of water, of fountains and springs, flowing out in the valleys and hills, a land of wheat and barley, of vines and fig trees and pomegranates, a land of olive trees and honey, a land in which you will eat bread without scarcity, in which you will lack nothing, a land whose stones are iron, and out of whose hills you can dig copper. And you shall eat and be full, and you shall bless the LORD your God for the good land he has given you. (Deuteronomy 8:1-10)

The *action* of battle is the voice of praise. The conflict belongs to the Lord and is His to fight. During the skirmish there is nothing you can do to help Him. How do you minimize anxiousness? Focus on the Victor, not the struggle. Drown out the sound of turmoil by shouting the praises of God. Since the action is vocalized praise, what *attitude* works best in the scuffle?

I love music, all kinds of music. Many find it hard to discover what style of music is my favorite. I regularly enjoy soft rock, smooth jazz, romantic ballads, traditional country, rousing marches, and intricate classics. Occasionally I browse through church hymnals and sing timeless melodies of salvation, especially songs of triumph.

When studying Greek in college, each class session started with singing old gospel songs in the foreign language. A class favorite was "Victory." A victorious heart was clearly needed for a passing grade. We were even once asked to sing the song during a morning chapel service. We must have sounded terrible; the class never received another invitation.

Has a sense of victory departed from your heart? If so, most likely you are walking very close to defeat. A triumphant attitude paves the way to winning. A prevailing spirit leads to success and is needed in the battles of life.

I was privileged to coach various High School volleyball teams for five years. A total of 117 matches were played involving 245 sets. Three of five end-of-season tournaments were won by the teams. The coaching experience ended with an overall winning average of 0.731. The program produced some amazing teams, including a couple exceptional players

During the rare occasion when a team lost a match, defeat always started in the heart. The players had plenty of physical ability and game skill to conquer any opponent. They became beaten by doubt and fear, causing them to quit playing passionately on the court. Often, a critically called time-out created the necessary mental adjustment. If the team lost, the look of defeat was on each player's face well before it showed on the scoreboard.

Similarly, a growing number of believers are showing signs of anxiety and frustration. How about you? Is your outlook on display through chronic complaining? Are you a time-bomb of exasperation? Are you finding yourself increasingly sarcastic? Have you figured out why?

Most likely a harmful attitude on a fleeting issue is creating discouragement, leading to disappointment. Followers of Jesus live by faith, not cynicism and criticism. God is eternally victorious, making trails where no path currently exists.

The Apostle Paul told Corinthian believers, "But thanks be to God, who in Christ *always* leads us in triumphal procession, and through us spreads the fragrance of the knowledge of him everywhere. (2 Corinthians 2:14) He was writing to a group of people not seeing many victories at the moment. One man was unquestionably living an immoral life. Believers were filing lawsuits on one another. Members were arguing over food restrictions. The taking of Communion was not lending itself to a sense of community. Spiritual gifts were being misappropriated.

The Apostle Paul, however, saw these battles from a victorious perspective. He sensed God would prevail in every struggle. With a prevailing attitude, he guided the local congregation to triumph.

A couple of events recorded in Scripture give some important insights about possessing a prevailing attitude in battle.

Egypt

How did the young man Joseph end up in Egypt? His brothers were envious of his special standings with dad and angry about a couple of dreams. They treated him contemptuously and sold him to slave traders. He became a victim of *child abuse* and could have easily become *bitter*. (Genesis 37)

As a slave, Joseph served a prominent family with integrity; his master profited greatly from his service. Yet he ends up in jail, falsely accused by the owner's wife. He became a victim of *injustice* and could have easily become *cynical*. (Genesis 39)

As a prisoner, Joseph encouraged a cellmate with a prophetical word. He simply asked to be remembered when the person was fully restored, but his kindness was forgotten. He became a victim of *neglect* and could have easily become *frustrated*. (Genesis 40)

Life was nothing but a battle for Joseph. How did he triumph when others would easily crumble? Twenty years later the secret became revealed, "God sent me here to preserve life…no one sent me here but God Himself…no matter what anyone did, God designed this situation as a saving moment." (Genesis 50) He faced battles with a prevailing sense of grace and mercy.

The problems, the setbacks, the hate, the scorn, and the ridicule were overcome by realizing God triumphantly leads. The experience was humbling, chastening, and disciplining, but he ended up prepared to rule with wisdom and kindness.

Joseph did not blame anyone but credited his situation to divine providence.

Wilderness

Why did Israel remain in the wilderness for so long? (Numbers 13-14) Twelve spies were sent to survey the land. Ten spies reported the place would devour them, the population being of great size. They advised friends and family not to attempt an invasion.

The response of the listening audience sounded like, "We hear your criticism, sense your defeatism and witness your frustration. Therefore, we would rather die than go any further." God responded, "You want to die? So be it! I sentence you to forty years of wasting away, one year for each day the spies assessed the current situation. Your corpse will lay buried in the wilderness."

The ten spies died immediately, and everyone older than 20 perished in the remaining years of wandering. Cynics and critics always die short of blessings.

What would happen if God was to place you into an upcoming battle situation? Would He witness a mindset of faith and victory? Would He see someone like the two faith-filled spies, Joshua and Caleb? Or would He observe grumbling and complaining?

Although the wilderness journey was punishment, God still attempted to make the experience spiritually beneficial, a long-term blessing.

The wilderness would be time spent in divine training, learning of strength through humility. They were taught trust and dependency. They discovered life is more than momentary situations, best viewed from an eternal perspective.

The wilderness was also a time of relational development, recognizing they had a special standing with God. They gained knowledge of genuine love, discovering the Lord chastens believers away from harm.

The wilderness was preparation, becoming more capable fighters. They ended up better able to correctly handle blessings. They discovered the Lord is with His people through thick and thin. They achieved a prevailing heart from the lessons of the wilderness and were triumphant in conflict.

On a June night in 1972, heavy rains flooded the Black Hills of South Dakota. A dam collapsed at a popular lake on the west side of Rapid City, overflowing the banks of the normally gentle Rapid Creek. Homes were destroyed by the immense force of the raging river. Hundreds of lives were lost. The carnage was massive and heartbreaking.

My wife and I immediately went back to her hometown to investigate her mother's well-being. We attended a Sunday church service. The pastor wanted to comfort and encourage the congregation. He gave time for believers to express their thoughts and feelings. A few emphasized faith and lovingkindness, but most gave comments of despair. A couple even grumbled against God.

Obviously, emotions are raw and fragile after a crushing experience, yet these kinds of events reveal the nature of the heart. Victorious moments *do* occur during devastation, but only those with a prevailing attitude are able to recognize them.

Prevailing

How is victory gained in the heart? First, develop a personal awareness of God's presence. Everything of lasting value is associated with the Lord. Unpleasant circumstances and situations will pass away. For those firmly residing in Christ, a ray of hope exists in every crisis. "And we know that for those who love God all things work together for good, for those who are called according to his purpose." (Romans 8:28)

Secondly, view life through the eyeglasses of eternity. As a follower of Jesus, everything evil that can possibly occur happens only in this lifetime. When all is said and done, believers enter an everlasting dwelling place with God and are winners forever and ever.

Whining

When living in Minnesota, the church building had some important structural issues and was in desperate need of a new coat of paint. God may look at the heart, but people prefer to first look at the outside. (1 Samuel 16:7) For friends and neighbors to discover His story, the facility needed immediate attention. No one was going to search for the Heavenly Father of beauty and splendor in a weatherworn dilapidated building.

The congregation was asked to give the painting project the highest priority and lend a hand whenever possible. Only one volunteer gave immediate attention. A public-school teacher put aside his normal summer job and joined me on the ladders every day.

Criticism, cynicism, and frustration began to surface in my heart. I could have really preached a barn-burner of a sermon, scorching everyone attending a Sunday service.

My co-worker modeled a triumphant heart, however. He focused on the additional people that would soon come. He expressed excitement about the numerous new families experiencing God for the very first time. From his perspective, there were no complaints.

The work was completed with both of us rejoicing about the future. Immediately afterward, attendance and finances improved. My four remaining years at this assignment saw continual growth.

Are you presently facing serious battles? Confront every skirmish with a prevailing attitude. Gain a sense of triumph in your heart. Before long you will see the victory.

CHAPTER SEVEN

PEACE

Now there was a famine in the land, besides the former famine that was in the days of Abraham. And Isaac went to Gerar to Abimelech king of the Philistines. And the LORD appeared to him and said, "Do not go down to Egypt; dwell in the land of which I shall tell you. Sojourn in this land, and I will be with you and will bless you.... And in your offspring all the nations of the earth shall be blessed, because Abraham obeyed my voice and kept my charge, my commandments, my statutes, and my laws." ... And Isaac sowed in that land and reaped in the same year a hundredfold. The LORD blessed him, and the man became rich, and gained more and more until he became very wealthy. He had possessions of flocks and herds and many servants, so that the Philistines envied him. (Now the Philistines had stopped and filled with earth all the wells that his father's servants had dug in the days of Abraham his father.) And Abimelech said to Isaac, "Go away from us, for you are much mightier than we." So Isaac departed from there and encamped in the Valley of Gerar and settled there. And Isaac dug again the wells of water that had been dug in the days of Abraham his father, which the Philistines had stopped after the death of Abraham. And he gave them the names that his father had given them. But when Isaac's servants dug in the valley and found there a well of spring water, the herdsmen of Gerar quarreled with Isaac's herdsmen, saying, "The water is ours." So he called the name of the well Esek, because they contended with him. Then they dug another well, and they quarreled over that also, so he called its name Sitnah. And he moved from there and dug another well, and they did not quarrel over it. So he called its name Rehoboth, saying, "For now the LORD has made room for us, and we shall be fruitful in the land." From there he went up to Beersheba. And the LORD appeared to him the same night and said, "I am the God of Abraham your father. Fear not, for I am with you and will bless you and multiply your offspring for my servant Abraham's sake." So he built an altar there and called upon the name of the LORD and pitched his tent there. And there Isaac's servants dug a well. When Abimelech went to him from Gerar with Ahuzzath his adviser and Phicol the commander of his army, Isaac said to them, "Why have you come to me, seeing that you hate me and have sent me away from you?" They said, "We see plainly that the LORD has been with you. So we said, let there be a sworn pact between us, between you and us, and let us make a covenant with you, that you will do us no harm, just as we have not touched you and have done to you nothing but good and have sent you away in peace. You are now the blessed of the LORD." ... That same day Isaac's servants came and told him about the well that they had dug and said to him, "We have found water." He called it Shibah; therefore the name of the city is Beersheba to this day. (Genesis 26:1-5, 12-29, 32-33)

The journeys of Isaac reveal a clear relationship between blessing and battles. Blessing can *create* battles.

The *action* of battle is the voice of praise: "The battle's ragin', but I'm still praisin'." God fights but believers dare not behave passively. The Lord is active in conflict and His people are active in praise. When praise is neglected, battles are lost.

The *attitude* of battle is a prevailing spirit. Believers lack endurance when a sense of defeat fills the heart.

In Air Force basic training, everyone had to

learn the proper procedure for reporting to superiors. New recruits are instructed to approach the door, give one firm knock, march in, stand at attention exactly two steps away from the desk, and give a sharp salute. A mistake during training rendered consequences.

During one practice session, all of us lined up in front of the sergeant's office door. Everyone was performing poorly and angry shouts by the drill instructor came from his office, *a sound of battle*.

Airman Harkness was right in front of me, waiting for his turn. He kept mumbling, "I know I can't do it; I know I'm going to get yelled at."

His moment to try finally arrived. Instead of making any kind of effort, he simply walked in and said to the sergeant, "Go ahead and yell sir, I know I can't do it."

The battle was lost because the sound of conflict got the best of him. He entered the effort without a triumphant heart. The result? The sounds of battle *intensified* and were now directed at him.

The Lord wins' battles with praise, and a conquering heart brings victory.

What is the right *approach* to battles?

Isaac was struggling with an action plan. The region was experiencing famine and he considered journeying to North Africa. Egypt represented a quick fix to a momentary problem. Years later, Israel would need deliverance from that very same nation, the enslaving grip of a short-sighted solution.

Isaac's temptation is just as common today. When life becomes dry and tedious, people quickly look for more pleasant conditions, wherever they may be found. God's warning to Isaac still should be applied: stay put, reclaim the promises, wait patiently, and gain more permanent results.

Temporary famines will be experienced when following Jesus but stay true to God. Avoid going back to old habits and ways. Embrace divine promises and anticipate their fulfillment.

Isaac went to where his father Abraham once resided; a place previously filled with wells of blessing. He discovered the waterholes had been destroyed. In ancient times, wells gave official claim of possession. The people were refuting family ownership, using intimidation to deny longstanding rights and privileges. Blessing sometimes includes the clashing of wills with others not rendering honorable service to God.

For Isaac to dwell on the site of ancient blessings

would mean trouble. He was willfully placing himself in harm's way. How does one approach something dangerous and possibly fatal? What tactic glorifies the Lord? What method produces righteous results?

Peace

Isaac pursued a peaceful existence. He did not desire disagreement or wish an argument. He was not looking for a fight; he was not craving contention. Yet, as God blesses His followers, others want what they have. Not something similar, but *what they have*. The potential for conflict increases.

Many falsely assume prosperity is only possible by having the exact same circumstances. If a person appears to have the *Midas touch*, others filled with envy inevitably believe, "If I had identical conditions, it would happen to me." Not true! Surrendering every personal decision and trusting God for the outcome brings success. Blessing follows faith, not jealousy and sulking.

Isaac understood what the Apostle Paul declared centuries later, "If possible, so far as it depends on you, live peaceably with all." (Romans 12:18) He knew blessings were directly linked to living for God.

The Lord helps people prosper no matter what they must relinquish, surrender, or abandon. Success is not based on circumstances, situations, conditions, or settings, but on conformity and service to God.

With a mindset of peace, he approached the squabble believing, "Take the well! That's not where my treasure lies, nor is it the source of my fruitfulness. Devotion to God and *peace with Him* is the root of my blessing."

Battles exemplifying the Lord are often not fought at all. Giving concession is frequently the evidence of God's blessing, the ultimate testimony of trust.

Submissive

When my children were teenagers, the movie "Princess Bride" was released. The film became a favorite in our home. The VCR version was played so much that it wore out. A DVD edition is now in our movie library.

The storyline begins with a young maiden dictating various commands to a farm boy. To each demand, he responded, "As you wish!" She eventually came to realize the response was more than a reply, but an expression of love. He won the battle, as well as her devotion, through submission.

During Isaac's attempt to reclaim family rights, he reopened wells, water being a precious commodity in the extremely dry region. Herdsman preferred giving milk instead of water to thirsty travelers.

When Isaac dug a well, an argument arose with local herders. With a mindset of peace, he moved on. At each additional well, a new quarrel developed. He graciously responded every time with something like, "As you wish!" Finally, he dug a well without contention and recognized the peaceful sign of divine blessing.

Isaac wanted a water supply, but not from just any source. He wanted springs of *living water* blessed by God.

Many promote: "Make things happen!" "Be a mover and shaker!" "Push hard and achieve success!" Contention caused by personal efforts, however, can be a sign that God is not blessing.

Are you praying, "Lord, bless what I'm doing!" and driving yourself into delirium? Or are you asking, "Lord, help me do what You're blessing!" and abiding in heavenly approval?

Isaac was submissive to the Lord, and the other herdsmen benefited. He walked humbly before the

God of Peace, not advocating quarrel and strife. When digging a well, if the results were not peaceful, he refocused and searched elsewhere. As soon as peace, a divine attribute, was part of the results, he quickly recognized God's presence and provision.

He said, "My Lord has provided room and He will make me fruitful." (Genesis 26:22) Pursue only where God is blessing.

Motives

After the battle, the Lord came in a special visitation to Abraham's son and renewed the divine covenant. Isaac personally became the recipient of the ancient blessing by achieving outcomes God's way.

Contrary to what many advocate, results are not everything. God is equally concerned in how they are accomplished. Motives should be constantly evaluated, not just conclusions. Blessings involve good endings, accomplished in godly ways. A clean conscience is a more accurate measurement of God's blessing.

Churches are often measured by crowd size, but people come for various reasons. Some are seeking God; others are only looking for entertainment or social acceptance. Churches are also measured by finances, yet some are financially comfortable by hoarding resources and failing to advance His story around the world.

Look to God for a different assurance of blessing: a favorable testimony by others. People notice the way results are reached. The herdsmen tried to discourage and hinder Isaac but later acknowledged the handiwork of God was witnessed in his behavior.

The approach of Isaac revealed he served the God of Peace, the One greater than obstacles. Fighting was not necessary. Anything blessed of God cannot be stopped; anyone blessed of God does not need to force outcomes. Results without God will not be pleasurable or personally enjoyed.

Taking life

A subject with diverse opinions deals with abortion, taking the life of the unborn. Even among those opposed to taking life, there are distinctions between *pro-life* and *anti-abortion*.

Some *pro-lifers* firmly oppose all forms of taking life.

Some *pro-lifers* oppose taking the life of the unborn but support eliminating the life of convicted murderers; they support capital punishment.

Some *pro-lifers* oppose taking the life of the unborn but support ending the life of someone painfully suffering a terminal illness; they support euthanasia.

Some *anti-abortionists* oppose taking the life of the unborn but support killing someone who regularly does the procedure; they support assassination.

The news media often puts these different convictions into the same category. The outcome? God is *praised* for defending the powerless, *accused* of double standards, and *blamed* for criminal behavior.

The issue of taking life clearly needs attention in society. The blessed outcome, showing the God of peace, is evident by seeing right results done in honorable ways.

Approach

The *action* in battle is a voice of praise, the *attitude* in battle is a prevailing heart, and the *approach* in battle is a mindset of peace.

If Jesus reigns in your life battles are not really your problem, they belong to Him. Walk humbly and submissively to the leading of the Holy Spirit, and let peace rule your behavior.

CHAPTER EIGHT

PERSPECTIVE

Finally, be strong in the Lord and in the strength of his might. Put on the whole armor of God, that you may be able to stand against the schemes of the devil. For we do not wrestle against flesh and blood, but against the rulers, against the authorities, against the cosmic powers over this present darkness, against the spiritual forces of evil in the heavenly places. Therefore take up the whole armor of God, that you may be able to withstand in the evil day, and having done all, to stand firm. Stand therefore, having fastened on the belt of truth, and having put on the breastplate of righteousness, and, as shoes for your feet, having put on the readiness given by the gospel of peace. In all circumstances take up the shield of faith, with which you can extinguish all the flaming darts of the evil one; and take the helmet of salvation, and the sword of the Spirit, which is the word of God, praying at all times in the Spirit, with all prayer and supplication. To that end keep alert with all perseverance, making supplication for all the saints.... (Ephesians 6:10-18)

Battles are a part of living in a rebellious world and God gives divine tactics to face them. Effectiveness in battle requires training, power, and skill.

Training involves studying Scripture: "Do your best to present yourself to God as one approved, a worker who has no need to be ashamed, rightly handling the word of truth." (2 Timothy 2:15)

Power comes by being filled with the Holy Spirit, immersed in His presence. Peter states, "You will receive the gift of the Holy Spirit. For the promise is for you and for your children and for all who are far off, everyone whom the Lord our God calls to himself." (Acts 2:38-39)

Skill is developed by experience. When serving in the Air Force, I was very proficient in the use of firearms. I received the sharpshooter award in basic training. At practice ranges on the island of Okinawa, I talked with other shooters, some seeing action in Vietnam. They all said the same thing: It is one thing to shoot at targets, but you really do not know your skill until in combat, when someone is returning fire. Conflict sharpens warfare skills.

The *action* in the battles of life is a voice of praise, the *attitude* is a prevailing heart, and the *approach* is a mindset of peace. What is the *arena*?

When engaged in a fight, people can easily lose sight of the actual battlefield, namely, anything connected to sin and rebellion. Sin is the ultimate struggle—sins of the body, inward nature, and speech. Action sins! Attitude sins! Audible sins!

Perspective is required in the battle arena. If a person loses sight of the enemy, they fight everything, even allies. Without a clear vision, someone can end up doing the work of the adversary.

When should battles be avoided? What battles should be fought?

The struggle is *not* with heaven

The war is not with others who follow Jesus. Taking issue with believers is a common practice but should be avoided.

Sometimes sincere followers of Jesus are accused of not being *spiritual*. Spirituality is frequently measured in superfluous ways. The concept is vague and ill-defined. Whenever a person's faith in God is brought into suspicion, insult and injury quickly occur, the wounds of battle.

Open conflict never produces heart change in others. The Holy Spirit has the key to every soul. Believers must work out their own salvation with fear and trembling. (Philippians 2:12)

The war is not with church leaders. Leadership involves watching over people's relationship with God. Some view these individuals as their worst enemy.

Leaders rebuke *and* restore, administer law *and* grace, by upholding righteous standards with merciful hearts. When people claiming to follow Jesus toy with their heavenly relationship, guardians of the soul confront and give an opportunity for a course correction.

People living for Jesus often talk of leaders in terms of *we* until their inappropriate behavior is addressed, then they talk in terms of *them/me*. "Who are *they* to talk to *me* about priorities and lifestyle?" A them/me mentality eventually leads to conflict, but shepherds are not the enemy of sheep.

The war is not with churches having the same beliefs. Speaking unkindly of an affiliated church never serves the Lord. Churches with different beliefs or people from other religions become confused by defamatory remarks.

I am credentialed with the Assemblies of God. The Movement is a voluntary cooperative group of ministers and churches that agree on sixteen basic beliefs. Each church is self-governing. They have chosen to enter into a mutual fellowship for training, global outreach, and accountability.

When regularly traveling as a guest speaker for higher education, I discovered additional beliefs were embraced by some churches beyond the sixteen fundamentals, a few viewpoints being debatable and causing personal discomfort. But the umbrella of the organization is large enough to cover, within the boundaries of established beliefs, supplementary ideas. The Assemblies of God *by design* has space for opinions that can lead to disagreement.

The war is not with other Christian churches. Diverse interpretation of Scripture has led followers of Jesus to treat other sincere believers as the enemy.

A few denominations lean toward *effortless apostasy* (easy backsliding) while others embrace *eternal security* (continued salvation despite defiant decisions and behavior). Also, various groups resist the Acts 2 experience known as the baptism in the Holy Spirit while others unreservedly proclaim the promise.

Do you refrain from contact or viciously oppose anyone not lining up with your personal position about faith in God? They are not the enemy.

Some badmouth the organized church, boasting independence. Free-spirited organizations and leaders can easily lose a grip on responsible behavior. Ironically, young people from these kinds of churches are often sent to an organized-church camp or retreat, as well as school and college. Organized churches provide many things independent churches struggle to offer.

Unconventional churches are occasionally criticized. Usually the bigger the church, the greater the scorn. Many of these fellowships are effectively and genuinely reaching unchurched people, sometimes better than conventional churches, fulfilling in unique ways the Biblical mandate to make disciples.

The war is not with para-church ministries. Sometimes faith-based humanitarian, medical, and educational organizations are accused of draining finances and volunteers from local churches. They are not the problem nor the enemy.

The war is not with the Lord. He is the dearest

friend of everyone and is not out to condemn anyone. Instead, He seeks to help. Genuine friends care enough to speak the truth while continuing to accept and support.

There once was an individual working in a public setting unknowingly struggling with body odor, causing others to dodge and avoid them. A sincere friend took the risk and courageously dealt with the awkward subject. Although the stinky person became upset and offended, those who speak lovingly and truthfully about obvious problems are not the enemy.

Everyone has some form of stench in their life. So, when God addresses your stink, the voice of the Spirit is not the enemy. The Lord sees the real you, meets the foul smell head on, and speaks about the need to take a shower in grace. He is not out to destroy but to establish you on the pathway of blessing. Placing God in the arena of your battle is a mistake.

The struggle is not with heaven.

The struggle is with hell

The war is with sin. The devil cannot be blamed for everything. Some temptations come from the satan, but people are just as tempted when carried away and enticed by their *own* lust. (James 1:14) In everyone is the root of sin; people do a very good job messing things up for themselves.

The rebellious and wayward nature occasionally surfaces. Major battles involve a misplaced heart, an unwholesome lifestyle, and a guilt-ridden existence. "Let us lay aside every encumbrance and the sin which so easily entangles us…." (Hebrews 12:1)

The war is with the spirit of the age. Becoming caught up with the lights and glitter of today does not take much additional focus or energy.

When my parents entered the retirement years, they went to San Diego annually to celebrate Christmas with my sister and her family. After my father died, everyone hoped my mother would continue taking the trip. I promised Mom that my wife, children and I would join her in San Diego to spend the holiday the first Christmas without Dad.

The trip from South Dakota to San Diego included passing through Las Vegas. I had gone through the city before and knew the cheapest place for a meal was in one of the more family-oriented casinos. They had a massive food buffet, away from the gaming area.

On our way back from San Diego, we arrived at

Las Vegas around mid-afternoon and decided to get a big meal, enough to satisfy hunger for the rest of the day. The family of six was stuffed to the gills for $15.

Our oldest son was still quite young and walked beside me to the dining area. He became fascinated by all the multi-colored lights—twinkling, dazzling, and alluring. He said to me, "Oh dad, this is a neat place."

I unexpectedly had a teaching moment. Pausing, I said, "Ignore the lights! Look at the blank and lifeless faces. Notice how many are wasting life on a stool."

Sad but true, many attempting to follow Jesus are engrossed with glamor. Multitudes are sitting on a stool, surrounded with flashing false promises, thinking nothing can be better. They have bought into an illusion.

The kingdom of God is a *counter-culture* of what the world offers, not a *sub-culture*. Look at the faces. See the lonely and empty lives produced by the spirit of the age. Believers are surrounded by people void of meaning and purpose.

The war is with the lucifer. There is a devil—the accuser of the brethren; the father of lies; the enemy of your soul. He exists, and with spiritual discernment you will regularly recognize his handiwork.

The devil is not out to get *you* but is seeking to wound *God*. He wants to see you fail because he knows how much it hurts the Heavenly Father. The satan is cruel and vicious, the ultimate deceiver and hater of all creation.

Whenever you yield to temptation, the lucifer laughs a sadistic cackle and throws your faults into the face of the Lord. By divine power, resist the devil and he will flee. Do not give an audience to evil. Walk away and be led by the Holy Spirit.

You are in an eternal struggle. The satan knows evil has lost but refuses to admit defeat.

Perspective

Recognize where your battle lies.

You wrestle not against other believers, church leaders, affiliated churches, other denominations, para-church ministries, or the Lord. Blend whenever possible, maintain unity, lift one another up in prayer, and walk humbly.

Your war is against sin, the spirit of the age, and the satan. Spend your energy fighting wickedness.

Many are wearing out spiritual resources fighting the wrong battle, doing more harm than good.

The action of battle is the voice of praise, the attitude is a prevailing heart, the approach is a mindset of peace, and the arena requires an accurate perspective.

Fight the hellish nature!

CHAPTER NINE

PROSPERITY

For he said, "Surely they are my people, children who will not deal falsely." And he became their Savior. In all their affliction he was afflicted, and the angel of his presence saved them; in his love and in his pity he redeemed them; he lifted them up and carried them all the days of old. But they rebelled and grieved his Holy Spirit; therefore he turned to be their enemy, and himself fought against them. (Isaiah 63:8-10)

From action, attitude, approach, and arena, the focus now turns to the *affliction* of battle.

Early in my church ministry, a teaching developed that followers of Jesus did not need to experience suffering. Various sources promoted if speaking a *right confession*, believers would be free from pain and poverty and be ushered into prosperity. In pursuing a clearer Scriptural understanding of suffering, I eventually wrote a magazine article entitled, "The Mystery of Suffering." Many readers greatly appreciated learning that suffering has a critical role in spiritual formation.

Whenever battles, conflicts, or adversity develop, people question various details about the Lord. A new convert commented to me, "With God in my life, I thought problems would go away. Isn't my life supposed to be smooth sailing from now on?"

Living for Jesus will make life smoother, not necessarily smooth. Momentary obstacles become more like the rolling hills of Tennessee than the majestic mountains of Wyoming. Everyday troubles, as well as the emotions attached to them, will continue to exist, just not as extreme as before.

Many rightfully embrace the notion of cause and effect and speak of sowing and reaping. Some situations may not fit the pattern. The truth of sowing and reaping must blend together with the sovereignty of God.

The Lord has been sovereign, is sovereign, and will always be sovereign. The earth is His ball and He makes the game rules. Thankfully, He is supreme goodness and establishes righteous values. Yet the providence of God never perfectly fits the mentality of highly self-focused people.

The Lord can and does move outside the realm of normalcy. When the unexpected ends up favorable, it is considered miraculous, a supernatural intervention. Should the Lord do something deemed personally uncomfortable, not as someone wants, anger is directed at Him.

Have you ever mumbled to yourself, "Unfair! God shouldn't act that way; that's not how it's supposed to be. He should work within systems I personally find pleasurable."

When facing a battle, do you question divine grace? His pure love is matchless, and broad enough to encompass conflict.

The reality of suffering

Adversity comes mainly because of three situations: Suffering occurs because of *personal wrongdoing*. Any form of affliction automatically prompts self-examination and evaluation. Believers often ask during agonizing moments, "Lord, have I done something wrong?" No doubt, wayward actions cause excruciating consequences.

When I regularly smoked cigarettes, various health problems associated with tobacco usage was gaining more public attention. After committing my life to Christ, I started reading the Bible. Scripture referenced the body as the temple of the Holy Spirit. I determined using tobacco greatly diminishes the glory of God. The only smoke filling a body should be the *cloud* of His presence. The addiction had to end. To continue would have been wrong, involving the dreadful consequences of poor health and possibly death.

Another reason for suffering is *unbearable wickedness*. Battles become necessary out of a sincere friendship with Jesus. Living for God in a rebellious world produces conflict.

When iniquity and injustice were wreaking havoc throughout Europe in the 20th century, Dietrich Bonhoeffer and Corrie ten Boom decided to aggressively resist the wickedness causing mass genocide. Dietrich was executed just days before the arrival of liberating forces, but his writings on the cost of commitment have impacted millions. Corrie became a dynamic servant of God, sculptured by the tension and strain generated by confronting obvious and blatant discrimination. A continent in conflict with evil prompted and outlined righteous reactions.

An additional reason for adversity has nothing

to do with wrongdoing or wickedness. Character and temperament need *refinement*, often formed by the hardships of suffering.

"And have you forgotten the exhortation that addresses you as sons? 'My son, do not regard lightly the discipline of the Lord, nor be weary when reproved by him. For the Lord disciplines the one he loves, and chastises every son whom he receives.' It is for discipline that you have to endure. God is treating you as sons. For what son is there whom his father does not discipline? If you are left without discipline, in which all have participated, then you are illegitimate children and not sons. Besides this, we have had earthly fathers who disciplined us and we respected them. Shall we not much more be subject to the Father of spirits and live? For they disciplined us for a short time as it seemed best to them, but he disciplines us for our good, that we may share his holiness. For the moment all discipline seems painful rather than pleasant, but later it yields the peaceful fruit of righteousness to those who have been trained by it." (Hebrews 12:5-11)

Even when doing nothing wrong, trouble can come by living right and abiding in the center of God's will. The Apostle Paul, *led by the Spirit,* found himself occasionally in trouble, experiencing cruel and harsh treatment. Difficulties do not necessarily mean being out of favor with the Lord or outside His good standings. With righteousness comes hardships, causing greater maturity that results in numerous eternal dividends.

Three reasons for adversity are personal wrongdoing, unbearable wickedness, and character deficiency.

Where is God?

When troubles surface, have you ever wondered if the Lord is the One fighting you? Do you toy with the idea that God is against you? The Lord is not the adversary. More likely the problem is a heart issue.

Isaiah wrote, "In all their affliction, He was afflicted," (V. 9) suggesting God agonizes with the hurting. The phrase can also be truthfully translated, "In all their affliction, He was not an adversary." God is not the enemy nor the blame.

Affliction brings stress and anxiety that distorts feelings. The pure joy of the Lord and His heavenly blessings easily become blurred or clouded over. The satan knows when someone is not thinking clearly and plays havoc with the imagination. He presents a false portrayal of the Savior and gives tempting thoughts, such as, "The Lord is your problem and is acting unfairly." Sadly, some believe devilish lies, concluding God is mean and requires appeasement.

Emotions are extremely unreliable during painful moments.

Where is the Lord? He is with you, experiencing the affliction. Abiding so closely, He is often unnoticed. During the worst moments, He will be found carrying you.

Our first assignment after college was in a wonderful church in Montana, a great pastor and compassionate congregation. The following summer, the pastor decided the time was right to take a new assignment. The normal practice back then was for the staff to also resign and look for another ministry opportunity. No wrongdoing or wickedness was involved in our circumstances. Although we would have preferred to stay, we saw relocation as simply the providence of God.

My wife and I started to make plans to move, but where? We thought about going to Seattle, my hometown. We considered heading to Rapid City, my wife's hometown. A couple of places contacted us about ministry positions, but they did not develop. Nothing went as we hoped. The pressure to provide for my young family was causing additional stress and strain.

With only a week left before moving out of our little parsonage, a job offer came from a glass company a hundred miles away. A kind and thoughtful pastor in the new location quickly found a duplex for us to rent and we made the transition.

Trouble only intensified. Not only was ministry suspended but there was very little income. Financially, we barely made ends meet. My wife creatively kept our two daughters clothed and provided nourishing home meals. Going to a restaurant was out of the question.

Initially, we went without a telephone. If extended family members needed to contact us, they called the pastor, who came and informed us. We then walked to a nearby phone booth and called them—collect.

I became discouraged and felt like a well-educated failure. Frustrated, I wondered, "Where are you, God? Do You want me in church ministry or not? *Why are you combating my efforts?*"

I had one thought right. The efforts were *mine*. I was not resting in the Lord and started believing God did not care. He must not be pleased with me; He is the One fighting me.

Feeling the tension of trouble, I considered God my adversary, clearly a character flaw in my life. My personal struggle drew out a defective outlook on abiding in Christ. The loving Heavenly Father used the pressure of the situation to mold me into a better servant-leader.

Regrettably, I pushed the pendulum to the other extreme, "Okay, God, if you don't want me in church ministry, I give up. I don't want it either!" I became convinced the Lord was out to defeat me. Instead, He was determined to destroy a deficiency in my soul.

The story of Joseph helped my recovery. When sold to slave traders, thrown into jail and forgotten, did he wonder if God was fighting him? Did he consider himself outside His will?

Joseph dealt with affliction by submission. He put the future in God's hand. Years later, he said to his brothers, "You meant it for evil, but God meant it for good." The public record of the young man's life testifies God's presence is experienced through submission and trust.

Thankfully, the Lord is patient toward His followers. In time, I resubmitted my life and calling to Him, His pleasure becoming my ambition. If He felt it necessary to suspend or end ministry, my satisfaction and joy were in just knowing Him. By yielding my troubled heart, the clouds of confusion rolled away. God was there all the time, opening and not shutting doors. He was positioning me for greater and more fruitful ministry.

Responding to adversity

How should a person respond to adversity? Isaiah records Israel *rebelled* in response to trouble. The result? God rose up against them. The Lord always addresses a rebellious reaction. The disobedient nation grieved His Spirit and the never-changing God challenged their efforts.

Submission leads to heavenly grace, while defiance leads to divine opposition. A mutinous heart causes God to rise up and give resistance. The *only* solution is submission.

Are you turning your back on the only One able to help? When every situation is given over to Him, despair rolls away and peace enters the soul.

Prosperity

The third reason for adversity is character flaws. Conflict brings followers of Jesus to a valley of decision, containing just two choices; rebel or submit. Submission brings the solution while rebellion triggers a confrontation.

The *action* of battle is the voice of praise, the *attitude* is a prevailing heart, the *approach* is the mindset of peace, and the *arena* requires perspective.

The *affliction* of battle ushers in genuine heavenly prosperity—a life liberated from the ramifications of adversity.

CHAPTER TEN
PRIORITIES

Since we were violently storm-tossed, they began the next day to jettison the cargo. And on the third day they threw the ship's tackle overboard with their own hands. When neither sun nor stars appeared for many days, and no small tempest lay on us, all hope of our being saved was at last abandoned. Since they had been without food for a long time, Paul stood up among them and said, "Men, you should have listened to me and not have set sail from Crete and incurred this injury and loss. Yet now I urge you to take heart, for there will be no loss of life among you, but only of the ship. For this very night there stood before me an angel of the God to whom I belong and whom I worship, and he said, 'Do not be afraid, Paul; you must stand before Caesar. And behold, God has granted you all those who sail with you.' So take heart, men, for I have faith in God that it will be exactly as I have been told. But we must run aground on some island." ... *The soldiers' plan was to kill the prisoners, lest any should swim away and escape. But the centurion, wishing to save Paul, kept them from carrying out their plan. He ordered those who could swim to jump overboard first and make for the land, and the rest on planks or on pieces of the ship. And so it was that all were brought safely to land. (Acts 27:18-26, 42-44)*

The narrative is about a prolonged tempest the emissary Paul experienced while heading to Rome. He was traveling to the capital city to make a formal appeal before the Emperor concerning a bogus complaint.

Storms have a couple of similarities to battles; both are barely controllable and must be managed to the very end.

During turmoil, do you attempt to deny the reality of the experience? A short ditty expresses the absurdity of such thinking: "There once was a man from Deal, who said that pain isn't real; yet when I sit on a pin, and it punctures my skin, I dislike what I fancy I feel."

Some seek comfort by blaming the devil for stormy experiences. Pointing a finger at a possible source does not form and shape a righteous life.

Everyone occasionally faces tough times, which is good. One of the great benefits is personal refinement. When turmoil is approached correctly they make you better, cultivating right thinking and sharpening critical skills. When approached wrongly they make you bitter, polluting and dulling senses.

Battles change outlooks; storms modify outcomes; conflicts alter conclusions.

A letter to the church in Corinth opens with, "Blessed be the God and Father of our Lord Jesus Christ, the Father of mercies and God of all comfort, who comforts us in all our affliction, so that we may be able to comfort those who are in any affliction, with the comfort with which we ourselves are comforted by God." (2 Corinthians 1:3-4)

The ability to comfort is acquired in situations where people become wounded and recover—during times of storms, battles, and conflicts. They better understand how to console and can more accurately give a reassuring word to others.

Up until my mid-twenties, I had never been hospitalized for anything. Then one day, doctors discovered tiny gallstones attempting to pass through ducts, causing extreme pain and requiring the surgical removal of the gallbladder.

I went under the knife with all the discomfort associated with the operation, gaining firsthand knowledge of what is and is not appreciated by visitors during recovery. My approach to comforting patients in hospitals was forever impacted. My painful experience made me a more astute comforter.

When my brother died, his final wishes and the actions of his wife intensified a greater sense of loss. The agonizing experience changed my approach to calming the bereaved.

The *abrasive* nature of storms wear on you until the weakest link in your armor is revealed, then the tempering of the thunderous ordeal strengthens your stamina. No one in their right mind wants the experience or joyfully enters the turbulence, but everyone can learn from them.

Three valuable lessons are learned by the abrasiveness of battles.

Jettison non-essentials

Battles cause a reprioritizing of life. Non-essentials once perceived as important appear useless during a storm. Turmoil teaches what baggage is extravagant and may cause sinking. People can live very well without many of the things marketers say are essential.

My wife and I have lived in several locations, moving numerous times. At first, we acted like pack-rats. After hauling *unopened* boxes from one house to another, we started lightening the load. We learned to remove unnecessary and unused possessions.

In storms and conflicts, staying alive becomes the only goal; you discover what is critical and what is not. In our home, during unstable financial times, various services and supplies became temporarily jettisoned, some were permanently eliminated.

Attached to every storm is a choice: Throw yourself or your cargo overboard. The sailors on Paul's ship threw over the baggage instead of themselves. Good idea!

My father drove locomotives all his life. A mile-long train, on average, takes two miles to stop. While hauling a load of freight, he noticed a woman trying to decide if there was time to drive over the rails. She drove onto the tracks, looked toward the train, and backed off. She did this a couple of times. Very bizarre behavior!

The last time she went on the tracks, the car engine stalled. At the last possible moment, she jumped out of her vehicle. The car was dragged down the track before the train could stop. When she got to the front of the locomotive, she repeatedly said, "My car, my car, my beautiful car." Finally, my dad quietly replied, "What about your life?"

In a split second, she had to prioritize. Many in similar situations prefer clinging to worthless titles, insignificant junk, and expendable objects. Everyone needs to be reminded of the difference between the real *important* and the invented *urgent*.

The stories of the old West include adventuresome settlers loading their Conestoga wagons with items they considered necessary for the future. Along raging rivers, treacherous mountain passes, and barren deserts the westward trails became littered with freight. Pioneers discovered the non-essentials of life during the journey. People still need to learn when to dump the stuff.

What is holding you back from successfully completing your journey? What is preventing you from triumphantly moving forward?

God is never late

The crew and passengers on the ship heading toward Italy eventually gave up all hope of being saved. The writer Luke, a traveling companion of

Paul, included himself on the list of those feeling hopelessness.

Storms are discouraging; they wear on *everyone*. People become emotionally drained, physically weary, and mentally fatigued. They may even lose a sense of equilibrium. Their *boat*, their normal every day stable composure, is uncontrollably rocking. And when people think they have had enough, the unrelenting storm keeps pounding.

When my children were young, we happily wrestled each other on the living room floor. There was one major difference between the daughters and sons. The girls would eventually want to quit and say, "That's enough, dad!" The boys just kept attacking and wrestling until I said, "Boys, that's enough!"

Have you ever said in a storm, "That's enough, Lord!" but the storm just keeps happening? In the stark reality of a storm, hope is easily forsaken. You find yourself crying out, "God, enough already!" Yet, He uses those moments to chip away unwholesome pride from stony hearts, as well as shameful arrogance and inflated egos. Very painful! Storms rage until detrimental and destructive qualities are destroyed.

While the sailors were on the deck discouraged

and thinking all was lost, Paul was receiving a message of hope in the belly of the ship. In storms, the Master of the sea has some form of intervention, maybe not as expected but highly effective.

The Lord holds time in His hands and is never late. He may not come when you want but always arrives on time. An island of rescue may appear at the last possible moment, perhaps coming up short of personal wants and wishes. Even so, an answer has come. When you think the situation is hopeless, keep looking to the horizon.

Prayer changes outcomes

Someone should have died in the storm. Prisoners were normally executed to prevent their escape. Non-swimmers were also on-board—some should have drowned. Death was the norm, but Paul prayed for life and the course of events was changed.

Without prayer, the outcome would have been tragic. Without calling out to God, the devastation would have been total and complete. During struggles and storms, petitioning the Lord brings divine involvement.

Most people know dialing 911 is important during a crisis. Built into the emergency system is a readout that gives the name, phone number, and address to a dispatcher as soon as a call is received. The caller might not be able to say what the problem is, or may be hysterically screaming into the receiver, but the dispatcher does not need anything from the person calling. They know where the call is coming from and help is on the way.

In moments of desperation and pain, people quickly make *disaster prayers*, sometimes hysterically. They often do not know what to say. God receives the prayer, knows the name and circumstance, and the answer has been initiated. The Helper is on the scene.

Storms cause people to pray. Unfortunately, some just pray when they have problems. If this is the only time when you pray, expect a lot of trouble. God wants everyone to pray regularly.

Priorities

Years ago, one of my writings was published entitled, "Dangerous Prayers." Unusual circumstances generated the magazine article.

I had been battling restlessness and frustration, pondering many of life's *why* questions—not *how* questions or *when* questions, but questions about the meaning of situations and circumstances. This inward struggle brought me down to the very purpose of existence—the significance of life, family, work, and how they interrelate. Priorities were being evaluated and the non-essentials of life were being jettisoned.

While experiencing this inner turmoil, I attended a week-long conference in Dallas, Texas. Before attending a training session on Wednesday morning, I prayed conversationally to the Lord in my hotel room. An out-of-ordinary thought unexpectedly flooded my mind. The contemplation did not fit my normal thinking patterns. The experience was not mystical, but mysterious. Throughout the day, correlating ideas came to mind and I jotted down notes, including the following two paragraphs:

"You have been praying for the Lord to expand your spiritual insight and you have been preaching that any place outside of your comfort zone is a place of expansion. The reason you are restless and frustrated is because God is answering your prayer."

"When being expanded, you are thrust to the very limits of faith. When at your limits, you come to the very edge of belief; you feel it would not take much to go over the edge. You have a choice: stretch or snap. That is what makes expansion frightening. At times, an unusual fear grips your heart. Because of the nature and feelings of expansion, many refuse to pray for spiritual depth and fail to grow."

Storms often bring restlessness, frustration, and fear. The abrasiveness of storms reveals the things that make success possible: get rid of sinkable non-essentials; know God has a workable solution; prayer will change disaster to achievement.

The *action* of battle is a voice of praise, the *attitude* is a prevailing spirit, the *approach* is a mindset of peace, the *arena* requires perspective, the *affliction* ushers in prosperity, and the *abrasiveness* impacts priorities.

CHAPTER ELEVEN

PARADISE

And my God will supply every need of yours according to his riches in glory in Christ Jesus. To our God and Father be glory forever and ever. Amen. (Philippians 4:19-20)

Battles involve action, attitude, approach, arena, affliction, and abrasiveness. The final focus is the *accomplishment* of battles.

Philippians gives a wonderful divine promise: The One who loves deeply and sincerely will supply the needs of His followers. He does this to the full and unlimited extent of His splendor.

Personal needs involve physical provision, mental condition, and spiritual formation. The ability to abundantly dwell on the earth, to gain wisdom and contentment, and to sweetly experience divine communion are completely addressed by the Heavenly Father.

God supplies every need, but His majesty is the focal point. Is He seen in your possessions, outlook, and countenance? If desires of the physical, mental and spiritual do not glorify God, they fit better in the category of *wants*. His grandeur and your *needs* work together and bring about righteous results.

Some essentials of life are only met through battles, conflicts, and storms. Paul commented, "For it has been granted to you that for the sake of Christ you should not only believe in him but also suffer for his sake, *engaged in the same conflict* that you saw I had and now hear that I still have." (Philippians 1:29-30) Although not a pleasant thought, some important attributes are developed through various struggles.

When in conflict, people are not always sure what is supposed to be learned. Have you ever prayed during turmoil, "Lord, what are you trying to teach me?"

My friend Owen Carr made this observation: "God's tests are not like school exams. In school, you select a subject, study the material, and take a test. Not so with God. In His classroom, He first gives the test, then explains the subject, and eventually reveals what was learned. After gaining knowledge from one lesson, He gives another test."

Three needs can only be met in battles, conflicts, and storms.

Grace through thorns

"So to keep me from becoming conceited because of the surpassing greatness of the revelations, a thorn was given me in the flesh, a messenger of Satan to harass me, to keep me from becoming conceited. Three times I pleaded with the Lord about this, that it should leave me. But he said to me, 'My grace is sufficient for you, for my power is made perfect in weakness.' Therefore I will boast all the more gladly of my weaknesses, so that the power of Christ may rest upon me. For the sake of Christ, then, I am content with weaknesses, insults, hardships, persecutions, and calamities. For when I am weak, then I am strong." (2 Corinthians 12:7-10)

What was Paul's thorn? Various suggestions have been given: a sickness, a physical handicap, a demon-possessed antagonist, an unwholesome desire, a hot-temper. What this implies is that *thorns* come in an assortment of appearances. Everyone can identify with Paul and with thorns. What is the *thorn* in your life?

Consider a rose. Seen in the sunlight are green leaves and beautifully-colored petals, but just beneath the beauty is something pointed and sharp, able to inflict pain and draw blood. There is an element of deceptiveness in a thorn.

Paul's thorn counteracted the fame, the accolades, and the favored revelations from God. Special moments with the Lord could have made him conceited. Pride would have made him useless. Paul needed to keep his thoughts about himself in a God-ward perspective. He needed to remember: "I'm not that great of a guy." To enable him to exalt the Lord and increase the revelation of God to others, he had something painful drawing humility out of him.

Paul discovered the sufficiency of the Lord. He experienced the truth that what genuinely thrills the human soul is a relationship with Jesus. He learned the greatest strength is found in weakness, depending solely upon God and embracing Him as the Answer.

Gordon MacDonald advocates the need of re-engineering spirituality, a refinement of how Jesus wants believers connected to Him. The current and upcoming generations need to understand what it is like to lay their lives on the line. Is the church going to survive and thrive? Not unless followers of Jesus reacquire an understanding of the words *humility*, *prayer*, and *sacrifice*.

I am not pleased with my behavior at the first church where I served after college. They were terrific people. Yet in my youthful idealism, I was overly sure of myself and was convinced I had all the answers. Youthfulness is not wrong (the church needs godlier zeal), but a negative downside is impetuous actions.

I thought every issue was critical, requiring me to exercise an imaginary pastoral *authority*. Every problem was intense, demanding my *firm* grip. I was in desperate need of humility, and God was faithful. What followed that brief ministry assignment was a season of re-engineering.

I came to the point of grieving so much over my initial approach to leadership that I contemplated sending a letter of apology. The congregation would not have understood. The entire time my family and I were with them, they graciously overlooked my faults and afterward had nothing but fond memories and kind regards.

Should you be expecting a thorn experience soon? Everyone needs a greater awareness of grace. Believers need to be reminded that salvation is a grace phenomenon—not self-achieved piety, self-made righteousness, or self-ingenuity. Followers of Jesus would do well to be knocked down a couple of notches, become self-effacing, and gain a more precise picture of God.

Attached to greater grace is a painful thorn.

Patience through tribulation

"For this very reason, make every effort to supplement your faith with virtue, and virtue with knowledge, and knowledge with self-control, and self-control with steadfastness, and steadfastness with godliness, and godliness with brotherly affection, and brotherly affection with love. For if these qualities are yours and are increasing, they keep you from being ineffective or unfruitful in the knowledge of our Lord Jesus Christ. For whoever lacks these qualities is so nearsighted that he is blind, having forgotten that he was cleansed from his former sins. Therefore, brothers, be all the more diligent to confirm your calling and election, for if you practice these qualities you will never fall. For in this way there will be richly provided for you an entrance into the eternal kingdom of our Lord and Savior Jesus Christ." (2 Peter 1:5-11)

Followers of Jesus occasionally say, "Whenever I pray for patience, things seem to get worse." That is how patience grows.

The Bible emphasizes the importance of perseverance (patience), requiring prayer to gain this attribute. Steadfastness makes for an assured entrance into the eternal kingdom.

Paul wrote, "Not only that, but we rejoice in our sufferings, knowing that suffering produces endurance, and endurance produces character, and character produces hope, and hope does not put us to shame, because God's love has been poured into our hearts through the Holy Spirit who has been given to us." (Romans 5:3-5)

Tribulation develops persevering power and an increase of strength in the Lord. One outcome is the ability to better combat toxic feelings, tedious problems and tiresome enemies. Better a little turbulence now then to experience the Great Tribulation soon coming upon the whole earth.

Divers wanting to expand their ability to stay below water force themselves to remain under until the pressure physically hurts. With every attempt the time gets longer. The magician Houdini practiced until he could hold his breath under water 12 to 14 minutes. Similarly, make every effort to expand your ability to persevere.

Growing up in a railroader's home, train workers demonstrated a very close bond. They were a tight-knit group. The annual locomotive engineers' picnic was a favorite family event.

When my father died, several old-timers came to his funeral service, showing their final respect. Afterward, they came to the house, sat together in the living room, and shared great memories. Many stories ended with, "The railroad is not the same today. The work is similar but not the workers. We were known as a brotherhood. Everyone worked to make the railroad work. Now everyone only watches out for themselves. They just put in the time, draw a paycheck, and quit if demands are too great."

Sounds like the church world, putting in the time and ready to move on if conflicts erupt and difficulties become immense.

The church has witnessed a sizable decline in enduring patience and persevering power—a diminishing of stick-to-it-iveness in the home, career, and faith. How is any kind of perseverance and endurance acquired? Through sheer determination while facing various trials.

Conflict is going to occur within faith communities. There is no escaping the fact that some people prefer to act as *the sore beneath the surface,* and others quickly look for *any excuse to leave.* Identifying harmoniously with a group of followers, and lending support to the worldwide cause of Christ, is critical to developing greater faith.

This may appear as a contradiction. I hope not. Leaders and believers should make every effort to work out differences, but if a congregation is determined to maintain a *bitter* disposition and refuse to advance, then gracefully leave and invest elsewhere. Wipe the dust off your feet and waste no further time with contentious people. Life is too short to spin your wheels serving in a bullheaded, unbending, stubborn, and crushing environment.

Victory through conflict

"For everyone who has been born of God overcomes the world. And this is the victory that has overcome the world—our faith." (1 John 5:4)

While growing up, my brother and I constantly wrestled. Being younger and smaller, I found myself on the bottom of the pile most the time. As a teenager, I started catching up in size and strength. As long as he could win, he challenged me to a brawl. Eventually, I could match him position for position and grip for grip. The final scrap ended in a draw. I felt victorious, and he never pursued another bout. The thought of losing to his *little brother* was too much.

Thank God for battles. If there were no battles, there would be no victories. Victory only comes through struggle.

Many personal faults and shortcomings are not given over to God without a fight. Some harmful habits are hard to overcome. Are you struggling with a nasty practice, a bad attitude, a destructive action? Are you questioning why some issues are gigantic while others are easy to overcome?

The magnitude of a battle assures all credit goes to the Lord after the transformation is attained. You appreciate the triumph more when the cost is sizable. Greater victory is consistent with great conflicts.

There is no victory without battles and no skirmishes without scars. The Son of God went into battle that left wound-marks on Him. Jesus will always be identified with *nail-scarred hands*. What makes you think you will get through a fight without a scratch? Expect some injuries.

Scars are nothing more than healed-over wounds. They may remain visible and seem unsightly, but they quit hurting in time. Scars remind you of what happened, but they only keep inflicting pain by picking the scab. Let it mend!

Prevention

Have you wondered if God *gave* the thorn, or *sent* the tribulation, or *created* the conflict you are experiencing? If He is genuinely your *Lord*, does it matter?

God loves you and whatever He orchestrates has your best interest at heart. He supplies all your needs and provides them in perfect ways. Battles are designed to address personal shortcomings, areas needing critical attention.

Sometimes people conclude God is not fair. Is it right to think the Lord is unjust when everything He does is to prevent you from eternal agony? Gain an eternal perspective: experiencing a measure of hell now is far better than everlasting damnation. A present-day pain may be the very thing keeping you away from the devastating results of separation from the Lord.

Believers need greater grace, patience, and victory; these are met by way of thorns, tribulations, and turmoil. Perseverance plus perspiration produces paradise.

The *action* of battle is a voice of *praise*; the *attitude* is a *prevailing* spirit; the *approach* is a mindset of *peace*; the *arena* requires *perspective*; the *affliction* brings *prosperity*; the *abrasiveness* adjusts *priorities*; the *accomplishment* is *paradise*.

EPILOGUE

"So will I save you, and you shall be a blessing. Fear not, but let your hands be strong." (Zechariah 8:13)

BONUS FEATURE
MOUNT OF BLESSING

At that time Joshua built an altar to the LORD, the God of Israel, on Mount Ebal, just as Moses the servant of the LORD had commanded the people of Israel, as it is written in the Book of the Law of Moses, "an altar of uncut stones, upon which no man has wielded an iron tool." And they offered on it burnt offerings to the LORD and sacrificed peace offerings. And there, in the presence of the people of Israel, he wrote on the stones a copy of the law of Moses, which he had written. And all Israel, sojourner as well as native born, with their elders and officers and their judges, stood on opposite sides of the ark before the Levitical priests who carried the ark of the covenant of the LORD, half of them in front of Mount Gerizim and half of them in front of Mount Ebal, just as Moses the servant of the LORD had commanded at the first, to bless the people of Israel. And afterward he read all the words of the law, the blessing and the curse, according to all that is written in the Book of the Law. There was not a word of all that Moses commanded that Joshua did not read before all the assembly of Israel, and the women, and the little ones, and the sojourners who lived among them. (Joshua 8:30-35)

The divine promise God made with His creation is revealed in stages through events involving Noah, Abraham, Moses, David, the Messiah, and the returning King; *one* covenant progressively revealed.

The name *Shaddai* was a favorite name of God in the older covenant. *El Shaddai* translates into "God of my mountain," possibly "God of might." Like the heights of a mountain, the Lord mightily reigns above everything.

Mountaintop experiences were also connected to the revelation of His covenant. At every point of discovery, an action was required on a mountain.

Noah and Mount Ararat: Get out of the ark. Trust God!

Abraham and Mount Moriah: Sacrifice name and reputation. Give God your future!

Moses and Mount Sinai: Follow divine directives. Live in purity!

David and Mount Zion: Represent the righteous King. Worship Him!

The Messiah and Mount Calvary: Give your all. Live crucified!

The returning King and Mount of Olives: Triumph over evil. Be fully restored!

Moses prepared the people entering the Promise Land with instructions from Deuteronomy, God's law to the conquering generation. They were to participate in a special mountaintop experience; half standing before Mount Ebal and half before Mount Gerizim. The event emphasized the covenant as a blessing and a curse (sowing/reaping; actions/consequences), a blessing if followed and a curse if rejected.

Jesus reiterated the bless/curse concept in the Beatitudes, as recorded by Luke: "Blessed are you who are poor, for yours is the kingdom of God. Blessed are you who hunger now, for you shall be satisfied. Blessed are you who weep now, for you shall laugh. Blessed are you when men hate you, and ostracize you, and insult you, and scorn your name as evil, for the sake of the Son of Man. Be glad in that day and leap for joy, for behold, your reward is great in heaven. For in the same way their fathers used to treat the prophets. *But woe to you who are rich, for you are receiving your comfort in full. Woe to you who are well-fed now, for you shall be hungry. Woe to you who laugh now, for you shall mourn and weep. Woe to you when all men speak well of you, for their fathers used to treat the false prophets in the same way."* (Luke 6:20-26)

Everyone and everything need God's blessing. His blessing must saturate the Church, congregations, ministries, communities, schools, businesses, families, individuals, and especially leadership. The world is starving for honorable and trustworthy leaders.

The classic book <u>Leadership Prayers,</u> written by Richard Kriegbaum, a leader in Higher Education, expresses heartfelt prayers for people serving in positions of responsibility. The prayers give attention to such things as reality, wisdom, hope, courage, values, and integrity.

One prayer highlights blessing. There are two sentences that are worth additional contemplation.

Success and blessing

The author wrote, "Help me to know the

difference between success and blessing." Believers often equate the blessing of God as similar to a successful venture. The measurement of God being involved in an activity, event, or organization is sometimes: How *successful* is it?

The church usually measures success the same as the secular market, via statistics. At Trinity Bible College, the Board of Regents regularly came on campus to review progress. The members wanted specific data—enrollment figures, new application numbers, financial reports. If enrollment, applications, or finances were increasing, then God was *blessing*. If enrollment, applications, or finances were declining, then a problem needed addressing so God could *bless* again.

Can people control, regulate, and *manipulate* His blessing simply by human ingenuity? Is blessing associated with *skill* or *obedience*? Scripture reveals blessing is connected to obedience.

Success is accomplished by *preparation* and *opportunity*. Some are prepared but never get an opportunity; others get the opportunity but are unprepared. When *preparation* and *opportunity* are effectively combined, the result is *success*.

The church world continues to be deeply engrained in a church growth mentality. Attendance, finances, and ministry participation are reviewed, and God is blessing when the figures are up. Is this true?

My wife and I were invited to New York City to spend time with Jim and Carol Cymbala, as well as David and Gwen Wilkerson. On Tuesday afternoon, in casual conversation, David said, "I don't pray for church growth." His prayers centered on holiness, purity, righteousness, and churches faithfully proclaiming Christ in anticipation of His coming. He prayed for the church's obedience—God's blessing.

Blessing centers on *fruitfulness*. Is the church bearing fruit—holy fruit, transforming fruit, life-changing fruit? What good is a well-attended church if people are not living rightly, if people are not fully engaged with Jesus?

In the Parable of the Vine (John 15), believers are instructed to bear *much fruit*. Does it matter how much foliage there is on the vine, or how beautiful a bush has become, if it is not producing fruit? Does it matter if a church appears corporately successful, having little or no spiritual formation?

Can a congregation be few in number and be blessed? Yes! Can a church with limited finances be blessed? Absolutely! Do not misunderstand: more people need to attend church. God has a *huge* assignment for His followers. People need the *message* of His community and a genuinely transforming *environment*. Size, however, is not the measurement of blessing.

Look at blessing from another perspective. In most cultures, the recognized abilities and skills of leaders in their late fifties start to lose value, they decrease in marketability. Elderly people are often perceived as *too old* to be viable candidates for employment, at least in higher-paying jobs. Many leaders end careers in insignificance, as measured by *success*. Does this mean they are not blessed because of not being pursued for prominent positions? Of course not!

Jonathan Edwards ushered America into a wonderful spiritual awakening. After leaving a renowned pastorate, he gave oversight for eight years to a small and remote congregation while serving as a missionary to the Housatonic Indians. During this time, he completed his celebrated work The Freedom of the Will.

Leaders, even with PhDs, having served with a high measure of success, sometimes walk away, by divine providence, from prestigious titles and return to the ranks of insignificance. The blessing is *bearing fruit* wherever planted.

Pleasant and unpleasant blessings

Kriegbaum also wrote, "Let me know your special favor, whether in your pleasant blessings or in the unpleasant ones. No matter what I may think of myself or what others may say...."

Some of God's blessings are unpleasant. The wilderness wandering people of Israel stood on the banks of the Jordan River being told the Promise Land would be a blessing, yet God's *blessing* would mean going to *war* with the Canaanites. Some Israelites were going to die in battle; homes were going to become fatherless; widows would weep over the consequences of the blessing.

Are opinions about blessings too narrow? Blessing can include conflict, hardships, and suffering.

When giving oversight to the Stone Church in Chicago Southland, a member had a nosebleed that would not stop. He went to an Emergency Room and they performed various test. One test revealed a spot on one of his kidneys. The kidney was removed, and the lab result showed a large and cancerous tumor. The surgery successfully removed all the cancerous cells. The nosebleed, not initially considered a blessing, proved to be a great blessing.

Corrie ten Boom helps protect Jewish people during WWII and is *blessed* with imprisonment. Out of the furnace of Auschwitz came a jewel of a woman.

Before the movie The Hiding Place was released in theaters, a small promotional film called Corrie was produced for churches. A teenage girl saw the film and told her mother she hoped to be a "neat old lady" like Corrie when she was old. Corrie experienced humanity's worst to be deemed a neat old lady. She received a blessing few can comprehend, one purified through the Refiner's fire. Out of horrible circumstances have come some of the greatest artworks, songs, poems, and books.

Reports are regularly given about the persecuted church around the world. People feel terrible remorse, and should, yet Jesus said, "Blessed are those who are persecuted because of righteousness, for theirs is the kingdom of heaven." (Matthew 5:10)

To equate blessing with *pleasure* is a tragic mistake. Blessing should be equated with *presence*, the presence of the Lord. A blessed life is not without conflict, struggle, or even worldly failure. God uses a variety of means to humble believers and *humility* is the doorway to blessing.

Not all blessings are unpleasant; most are sweet

and satisfying. Psalms 147:1 declares, "How good it is to sing praises to our God, how pleasant and fitting to praise Him!" One of the more pleasurable experiences in life is gathering with others and praising His name. You sense, in greater measure, the blessing of His presence and the sweetness of His fellowship when singing to the Lord.

Ultimately, the blessing is walking with Jesus, regardless the road.

The signs of blessing

Joshua 22:5 reveals blessing as, "To love the Lord your God, to walk in all his ways, to obey His commands, to hold fast to Him and to serve Him with all your heart and all your soul."

Give two phrases special attention: "walk in all His ways" and "obey His commands;" the statements are not the same. Walking in His ways is responding to the *personal directions* of the Spirit; obeying His commands is practicing the *declared directives* of Scripture. Adhering to His personal directions *and* declared directives are signs of blessing.

Judges 2:19 reveals the opposite, "They *refused* to give up their evil practices and stubborn ways." Improper activities, actions, and attitudes (*evil practices*), as revealed in Scripture, remove God's presence and blessing, such as, sexual impurity, greed, idolatry, lying, coveting, gossiping, cheating, and discord.

Being unbending and having an unwillingness to move in His personal plan (*stubborn ways*) also removes God's presence and blessing. D.V. Hurst told a group of ministers, "Blessed are the flexible for they shall never break." Recognize the futility of rigidity. Stubbornness may be the number one cause for people not experiencing God's blessing.

Blessing

Embrace these two simple truths: There is a difference between success and blessing—you *need* blessing! And God's blessing is occasionally unpleasant—the end product is sweetness in your soul.

[Published: Enrichment Magazine, Spring, 2014, by the author]

ACKNOWLEDGEMENTS

I was blessed with several teams of capable credentialed ministers, joining arms together through sundry battles. They rose up victoriously and fought the good fight of faith.

SOUTH DAKOTA

Dean and Lynn Scott

NORTH DAKOTA

Dan and Phyllis Kuno, Roger and Annette Willis, Paul and Tracy Hamelink, Dayton and Marilyn Kingsriter, Keith and Sally Agree, David and Mary Jones

ILLINOIS

Mount Prospect

Jim and Jill Nichols, Todd and Debbie Forrest, Rich and Jane Weller, Joe and Shirley Broussard, Russ and Ginger Bechtold, Joe and Angela Bowman, Ron and Debbie Ross, John and Cindy Cosmos, Jeff and Jenny Smith

Palos Heights

Joe and Angela Bowman, Dug and Rebecca Harris, Erik and Bethany Scottberg, Tom and Sheila Salagaj, Paul and Franca Melidona, John and Marlene Schwider,

Duane and Sharon Swanson, Phil and Chanda Hahn,
Ken and Christine Darnell

Thank you for the blessing of your leadership. You proved abundantly able to handle the difficult battles in your assigned area of expertise.

ABOUT THE AUTHOR

Bob was born and raised in the Pacific Northwest. While serving in the Armed Forces during the Vietnam era, he met his wife, Brenda. They have lived in seven States and raised their four children mostly in the greater Chicago area. They presently reside in southern Missouri.

His career has been as a church overseer, a college administrator, a church denomination leader, a classroom instructor, an athletic coach, and an international emissary.

Bob is an ordained minister, as well as a nationally accredited high school volleyball coach. He is passionate for all generations to enter a life-changing relationship with God and having a fully integrated life through Christ.

He continues to write, teach, and speak in various settings. To view more of his current reflections, his blogs can be found at bob-maddox.blogspot.com. His other ten books are available online.

S. ROBERT MADDOX

BOOKS BY THE AUTHOR

SPIRIT Living, *abundantly following Jesus*

GOD, *who are You? Reflections from the names of God in the Bible*

TEN Words, *Reflections from the Ten Commandments*

BLESSING and battles, *Reflections on the Blessing of God and the Battles of Life*

ACTION, *Reflections from the gospel of Mark*

The **CHURCH**, *Reflections from Paul's letter to the Ephesians*

practical **FAITH**, *Reflections from James' letter to the Church*

pure **LOVE**, *Reflections from John's first letter to followers of Jesus*

COMFORT, *Reflections from Paul's second letter to the Corinthians*

really **READY**, *Reflections from the prophetic book of Daniel*

Available in Hardback, Paperback, and eBook editions.

www.ingramcontent.com/pod-product-compliance
Lightning Source LLC
Chambersburg PA
CBHW071504040426
42444CB00008B/1486